Private Capital Flows to Africa: Perception and Reality

Forum on Debt and Development (FONDAD)

Fondad is an independent policy research centre and forum for international discussion established in the Netherlands. Supported by a worldwide network of experts, it provides policy-oriented research on a range of North-South problems, with particular emphasis on international financial issues. Through research, seminars and publications, Fondad aims to provide factual background information and practical strategies for policy-makers and other interested groups in industrial, developing and transition countries.

Director: Jan Joost Teunissen

Nils Bhinda, Jonathan Leape
Matthew Martin, Stephany Griffith-Jones
with Country Teams led by Louis Kasekende,
Charles Kimei, Stuart Kufeni
and Austin Matale

Private Capital Flows to Africa

Perception and Reality

FONDAD
The Hague

ISBN: 90-74208-15-0

The views expressed in this book do not necessarily represent those of the Forum on Debt and Development.

This publication was made possible thanks to the support of the Ministries of Foreign Affairs of Denmark and Sweden, ING Barings, the Department for Development Cooperation of the Dutch Ministry of Foreign Affairs, and Novib.

Additional copies may be ordered from FONDAD at
Noordeinde 107 A, 2514 GE The Hague, the Netherlands
Tel: 31-70-3653820 Fax: 31-70-3463939 E-Mail: Forum_FONDAD@wxs.nl

Contents

Boxes

Tables

Figures

About the Authors

Central Team

Matthew Martin is Director of External Finance for Africa (EFA) and Debt Relief International (DRI) in London, which is working with over 15 African and Latin American governments, donor governments and international institutions on debt, external and domestic financing, and adjustment policy. He is responsible for the overall editing of the book, and joint author of Parts 1, 2 and 4.

Stephany Griffith-Jones is Senior Fellow at the Institute for Development Studies at the University of Sussex. She has led many research projects on debt and private capital flows, and advised governments in Eastern Europe and Latin America. She is joint author of Parts 1 and 2 of the book.

Jonathan Leape is Director of the Centre for Research into Economics and Finance in Southern Africa (CREFSA) and Lecturer in Economics at the London School of Economics, and was leader of the South African team. He has worked extensively on cross-border capital flows, debt management and foreign exchange intervention. He is author of Part 3, and joint author of Part 4.

Nils Bhinda is project manager at EFA and DRI, working on private capital flows and macro policy in Africa, and debt sustainability analysis for HIPCs. He is joint author of Parts 1 and 2.

South African Team

Lesetja Kganyago, Ministry of Finance, South Africa.
Yougesh Khatri, Economist, Africa Department, IMF. Formerly Research Officer, CREFSA, LSE, London.
Ernie van der Merwe, Economic Advisor to the Governor, Reserve Bank of South Africa.

Tanzanian Team

Charles Kimei (Team Leader), Managing Director, CRDB (1996). Formerly Director, Bank Supervision, Bank of Tanzania.
Godwin Mjema, Lecturer, Economic Research Bureau, University of Dar-es-Salaam.
Anna Msutze, MEFMI. Formerly Deputy Debt Director, Bank of Tanzania.
Ben Tarimo, on secondment to the World Bank office in Dar-es-Salaam. Formerly Deputy Director, Balance of Payments, Bank of Tanzania.

Ugandan Team

Louis Kasekende (Team Leader), Executive Director, Research and Policy, Bank of Uganda.
Damoni Kitabire, Director, Budget, Ministry of Finance.
Eric Mukasa, Strategic Planning Department, Ministry of Planning and Economic Development.
David Sajjabi, Senior Economist, Research Department, Bank of Uganda.

Zambian Team

Austin Matale (Team Leader), Assistant Director, Financial Markets, Bank of Zambia.
James Matale, Consultant. Formerly Director of the Zambia Privatisation Agency.
Inyambo Mwanawina, Senior Lecturer, Economics Department, University of Zambia.
Jerome Mweetwa, Manager, Investment Promotions, Zambia Investment Centre.

Zimbabwean Team

Stuart Kufeni (Team Leader), Director of Financial Markets Division, Reserve Bank of Zimbabwe.

Obed Matshalaga, Deputy Secretary, Domestic and External Finance, Ministry of Finance.

Rose Mazula, formerly Director of Policy and Research, Zimbabwe Investment Centre.

Rose Mkwebu, Assistant Director, Economic Research Division, Reserve Bank of Zimbabwe.

Moris Mpofu, Senior Economist, Economic Research Division, Reserve Bank of Zimbabwe.

We are very grateful to Kathy Wormald for her invaluable work in managing the project's finances, the administration, and in organising the closing workshop.

Abbreviations

ADB	African Development Bank
AERC	African Economic Research Consortium
BESA	Bond Exchange of South Africa
BIS	Bank for International Settlements
BOPSY	Balance of Payments Statistics Yearbook (IMF)
BOT	Bank of Tanzania
BOU	Bank of Uganda
BOZ	Bank of Zambia
BWI	Bretton Woods Institution
CDC	Commonwealth Development Corporation
CFD	Caisse Française de Développement
CMA	Common Monetary Area
CMSA	Capital Markets and Securities Authority (Tanzania)
CREFSA	Centre for Research into Economics and Finance in Southern Africa (LSE)
EAC	East African Community
EADB	East African Development Bank
EFA	External Finance for Africa Group
EIU	Economist Intelligence Unit
EM	Euromoney
ESA	Eastern and Southern Africa
FCA	Foreign Currency Account
FISCU	Finance and Investment Sector Coordinating Unit (SADC)
GDDS	General Data Dissemination System (IMF)
GFCF	Gross Fixed Capital Formation
HIPC	Highly Indebted Poor Country
ICSID	International Convention on the Settlement of Investment Disputes
IDS	Institute for Development Studies (University of Sussex)
IFC	International Finance Corporation
IFI	International Financial Institution
II	Institutional Investor
IMF	International Monetary Fund
JSE	Johannesburg Stock Exchange
MEFMI	Macroeconomic and Financial Management Institute of Eastern and Southern Africa
MIGA	Multilateral Investment Guarantee Authority
OECD	Organisation for Economic Cooperation and Development
RBZ	Reserve Bank of Zimbabwe
SACU	Southern African Customs Union
SADC	Southern African Development Community
SAP	Structural Adjustment Programme
SARB	South African Reserve Bank
SDDS	Special Data Dissemination Standard (IMF)
SSA	Sub-Saharan Africa
TIC	Tanzania Investment Centre
UIA	Uganda Investment Authority
UNCTAD	United Nations Conference on Trade and Development
USAID	United States Agency for International Development
ZCCM	Zambia Consolidated Copper Mines
ZIC	Zimbabwe Investment Centre

Introduction

Why study private capital flows to Sub-Saharan Africa? For the last two decades, international financial markets have perceived most of Africa as a "basket case" region. When the research underlying this book began (in 1996), donors, international organisations, investors and even African governments did not believe that private flows to Africa were significant or increasing.

Yet senior African government officials from 14 African countries, and especially South Africa, Tanzania, Uganda, Zambia and Zimbabwe, were telling a different story. They knew that a surge of flows to emerging markets, and the liberalisation of their economies, were prompting unprecedented inflows of private capital. These flows — and their occasional sharp reversals — were having dramatic macroeconomic effects and demanding urgent policy responses. But with few data on the level or composition of these flows, and no thorough analysis of their causes and effects, African governments were virtually powerless to react. It is their convictions and hard work which have made this book possible. The Swedish and Danish governments had the sense to listen to them, and we are also most grateful for their sponsorship of this research.

In setting out to explore and explain the dichotomy between international perception and African reality, we had to use an innovative methodology. Most of the literature on private capital flows has used international data sets to analyse their scale, composition, causes, sustainability, macroeconomic effects and policy responses, using largely econometric methods. It has focussed particularly on the so-called external or "push" factors which motivate the flows — mainly US interest rate trends and subjective sentiment-based factors in international markets (for a more comprehensive literature survey see Martin, Griffith-Jones, Kasekende and Kitabire 1995).

We realised rapidly that international data sets were not tracking the increase in private flows to Africa, and that most of their causes were region- or country-specific. Therefore the bulk of our research was undertaken by teams of senior government officials in five African countries. They collected local data and analysed the scale and composition of private capital flows, their locally-driven causes and sustainability, their macroeconomic impact, and the policy measures needed to influence their future scale, composition and effects on the economy. In addition, the central team conducted more than 150 interviews with major providers of private capital (investors, bankers and fund managers) in the UK and Africa, as well as international experts in the IMF, World Bank, UNCTAD and Commonwealth Secretariat and senior academics, to identify the "supply" side factors — international trends and perceptions of Africa — which have a major influence on the flows.

This resulting book is organised in four sections.

Part 1 (The Scale and Monitoring of Capital Flows) presents the facts on the scale and composition of private capital flows to Africa and the difficulties in monitoring them. It confirms the views of African policymakers — that flows are increasing sharply, and that foreign direct and portfolio investments are large relative to their economies, and therefore of critical concern in formulating economic policy. It explains how difficulties in measuring and monitoring flows (compounded by the liberalisation of controls) have led to substantial under-reporting of flows to the international organisations.

Part 2 (Perception and the Causes of Flows) looks at what motivates people to invest. It is based on surveys of more than 150 investors, in their home countries or in African recipient countries. It describes why they are increasingly diversifying FDI and portfolio flows (both geographically and sectorally), but warns against their potential volatility. It details the factors preventing medium-term bank lending (notably the continuing debt overhang), and describes why short-term bank flows are rising. It shows that flawed credit ratings short-change the region. Throughout, it finds that the best-informed investors are increasing their holdings, while the less informed are not.

Part 3 (Reality: Impact and Policy Responses) focuses on the macroeconomic impact and policy implications of capital flows. Drawing on the data and analysis presented in the country studies, together with the recent international literature, the analysis contrasts the generally positive impact on investment and growth with the destabilising effects on monetary policy and interest rates, the real exchange rate and financial markets. The chapter on policy responses highlights the urgent need to manage the sequencing of reforms more effectively, and to adopt a broader range of policy instruments to influence the impact of flows on the economy.

Part 4 (Conclusions and Recommendations) identifies measures which will help African governments to attract more development-oriented private flows, and to manage the economic impact of growing and more volatile flows. By introducing these measures, governments will encourage a wider group of potential investors to ignore superficial perceptions and to make their decisions more objectively, and enable international institutions and donors more successfully to promote flows to Sub-Saharan Africa. At

14

the same time, they will help to prevent destabilising effects on their economies and to enhance the positive impact on investment and growth.

African governments, donors and the international community can all act to make flows more sustainable and less volatile. Insofar as many African countries are suffering cuts in aid flows and need to mobilise large private flows, and nearly all have suffered from the instability of private flows, this book should be of interest to anyone concerned about the role of private capital in Africa's future development.

However, this book also has lessons beyond Africa. Since the "Asian Crisis" of 1997, international financial institutions and investors have been obsessed with the need for greater "transparency" in information provision by developing countries, which is often seen as a panacea for stabilising flows. But this book shows that gathering information on private capital flows is not easy, and that — as many developed countries with excellent information flows have found — complex investor perceptions rather than objective data guide most investment decisions. The macroeconomic effects of the flows and the appropriate policy responses are equally multi-faceted.

Emerging market governments (and the donors or international organi-sations which support them) need to realise that, though they can identify objective factors which attract "desirable" or "long-term" capital flows, growing integration into international financial markets is likely to exacer-bate the volatility of such flows. This increased volatility heightens the need for an expanded range of policy tools to enhance the positive eco-nomic impact of private flows and to avoid repeating the recent instability suffered by so many emerging economies. By presenting the first systemat-ic analysis of the recent African experience with private capital flows, this book aims to provide a rich source of new ideas for rapid policy responses by national and international policymakers.

Part 1

The Scale and Monitoring of Capital Flows

Chapter 1 Scale and Monitoring

Nils Bhinda, Stephany Griffith-Jones and Matthew Martin

1.1 Introduction

All types of private capital flows to Sub-Saharan Africa (SSA) have been increasing rapidly in the 1990s. All sources (whether international organisations or African governments) share this conclusion, though international sources disagree about the scale of the rise (Table 1.1). Apart from

Table 1.1 **Private Capital Flows to Sub-Saharan Africa: Comparison of International Data Sets**
(millions of dollars)

	1990	1991	1992	1993	1994	1995	1996	1997
FDI								
UNCTAD	1,132	2,078	1,547	2,049	3,667	4,792	4,275	4,604
Portfolio Equity								
IMF	4	-852	-799	882	231	1,477	1,426	-
World Bank	0	0	144	174	860	4,868	2,012	1,507
Bank (MLT net)								
BIS / OECD	814	-2,568	-1,100	-1,400	-1,100	-400	600	4,000
IMF	5,400	700	2,500	1,300	1,700	1,700	-900	-
World Bank	-762	85	-1,104	261	-503	-458	-1,996	-1,399
Bonds								
IMF	-264	486	2,548	260	1,507	1,420	1,211	-
World Bank	-941	215	237	-30	1,473	851	586	1,193

Notes and Sources:
FDI: UNCTAD World Investment Report 1996-8 (SSA total is calculated as "Other Africa" plus South Africa).
Portfolio Equity: World Bank, *Global Development Finance 1999*; IMF, Balance of Payments Statistics Yearbook 1997, Tab B-28.
Bank: IMF, World Economic Outlook 5/97; World Bank, *Global Development Finance 1999* (1991-7 data) and *Global Development Finance 1998* (1990) - MLT only; BIS / OECD Statistics on External Indebtedness: Bank and Trade-Related non-Bank External Claims..." various issues (ST and MLT).
Bonds: World Bank, *Global Development Finance 1999* (1991-7 data) and *Global Development Finance 1998* (1990); IMF, Balance of Payments Statistics Yearbook 1997, Vol.2, Tab B-29.

Zambia, all of our project countries have been major beneficiaries, with sharp recent rises for Tanzania, Uganda, South Africa and Zimbabwe. In absolute terms, South Africa receives more dollars than the other four countries together. However, relative to GDP, the other countries have levels (10-15%) as high as the fastest growing Southeast Asian and Latin American countries, while South Africa receives only 4%.

Agreement on general trends hides major discrepancies between different data sets. Several international institutions publish data, but these often wildly misstate flows or their composition, as they are based on a small number of national data sources. Behind these discrepancies lie problems at two levels. First, the international organisations often face major problems in assembling national data on time and interpreting their presentation. Second, African countries also face great problems in constructing consistent, comprehensive or timely databases.

Data from national sources show a somewhat different picture. As seen in Figures 1.1a-e, all the project countries show sharp rises in private capital inflows since 1993-4, although in the case of Zimbabwe the rises were fully offset by falls in 1996-7.

This chapter reveals the scale and composition of flows to Sub-Saharan Africa by comparing international and national databases, and highlights the key problems faced by countries and international organisations in producing data.

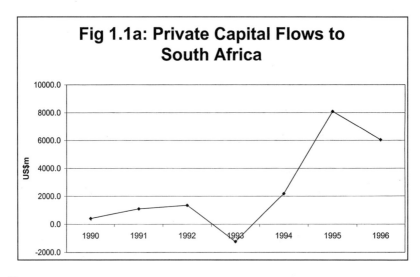

Fig 1.1a: Private Capital Flows to South Africa

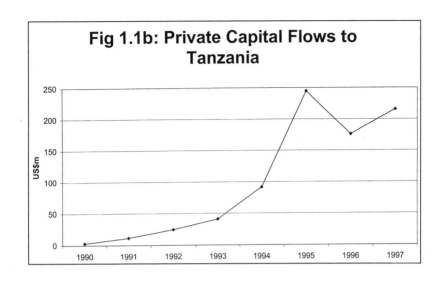

Fig 1.1b: Private Capital Flows to Tanzania

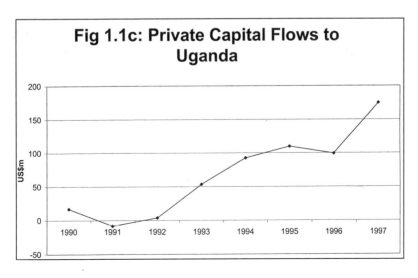

Fig 1.1c: Private Capital Flows to Uganda

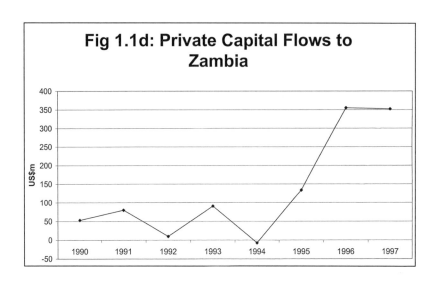

Fig 1.1d: Private Capital Flows to Zambia

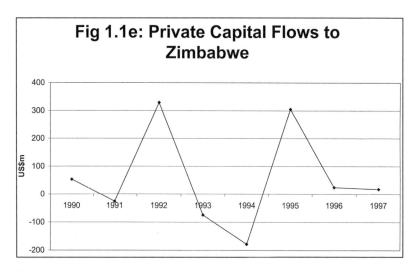

Fig 1.1e: Private Capital Flows to Zimbabwe

1.2 The Scale and Composition of Flows

1.2.1 Foreign Direct Investment (FDI)

As UNCTAD (1998) shows, Sub-Saharan Africa participated in the global surge of FDI to developing countries in the mid-1990s. Flows more than tripled between 1992 and 1995, exceeding the growth rates of other developing regions (Table 1.1).

Because it started at a low absolute level, Sub-Saharan Africa continues to receive a low share of total flows to developing countries (Figure 1.2). However, its inflows are highly significant as a proportion of gross fixed capital formation (GFCF) or GDP. UNCTAD data show ratios to GFCF way above averages for Latin America, Asia and all developing countries since 1993 (Figure 1.3a), and that Uganda, Zambia, and most recently Tanzania are above the SSA average (Figure 1.3b). When national data are used, this ratio becomes even higher for South Africa, Zambia and Zimbabwe (Table 1.2).

UNCTAD data indicate that, while flows to oil exporters (Angola, Cameroon, Congo, Gabon, and Nigeria) have increased significantly, their share of total flows to the region has declined due to massive increases for South Africa. As shown in Figures 1.4a-b, South Africa's share rocketed to 37% in 1997. Flows to the least developed countries (apart from Angola) have also increased dramatically — trebling since 1991.

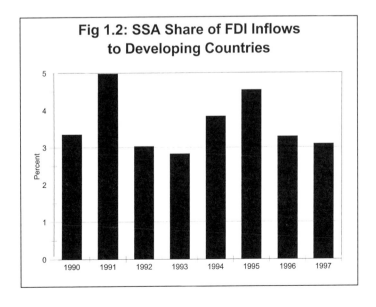

Fig 1.2: SSA Share of FDI Inflows to Developing Countries

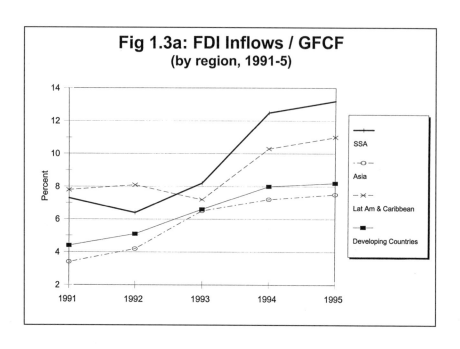

Fig 1.3a: FDI Inflows / GFCF
(by region, 1991-5)

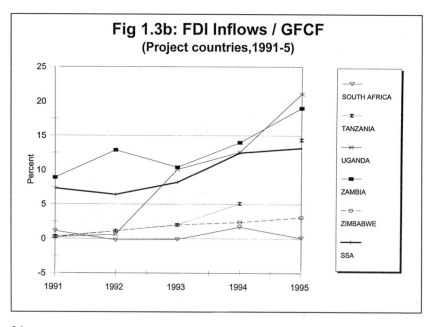

Fig 1.3b: FDI Inflows / GFCF
(Project countries,1991-5)

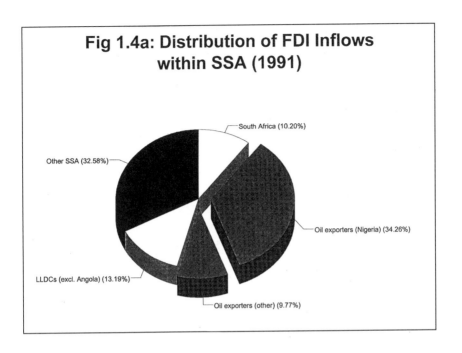

Fig 1.4a: Distribution of FDI Inflows within SSA (1991)

- South Africa (10.20%)
- Other SSA (32.58%)
- Oil exporters (Nigeria) (34.26%)
- LLDCs (excl. Angola) (13.19%)
- Oil exporters (other) (9.77%)

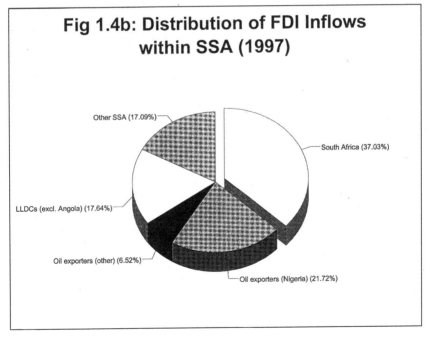

Fig 1.4b: Distribution of FDI Inflows within SSA (1997)

- Other SSA (17.09%)
- South Africa (37.03%)
- LLDCs (excl. Angola) (17.64%)
- Oil exporters (other) (6.52%)
- Oil exporters (Nigeria) (21.72%)

Table 1.2 Data Comparison of FDI Inflows (1990-98)
(millions of dollars)

	1990	1991	1992	1993	1994	1995	1996	1997	1998
South Africa									
Country data	-69.7	184.7	-24.5	-14.7	295.1	981.0	760.4	-	-
UNCTAD	-5.0	212.0	-42.0	-19.0	338.0	918.0	760.0	1705.0	-
Tanzania									
Country data	-3.0	3.0	10.8	16.9	49.1	168.9	148.0	157.0	172.0
UNCTAD	-3.0	3.0	12.0	20.0	50.0	120.0	150.0	250.0	-
Uganda									
Country data	0.0	1.0	3.0	54.6	88.2	121.2	121.0	175.0	210.0
UNCTAD	-6.0	1.0	3.0	55.0	88.0	121.0	121.0	250.0	-
Zambia									
Country data	203.0	34.0	50.0	55.0	40.0	97.0	117.1	125.4	-
UNCTAD	203.0	34.0	45.0	52.0	56.0	67.0	58.0	70.0	-
Zimbabwe									
Country data	-12.2	2.8	15.1	31.5	29.9	104.3	35.0	75.0	-
UNCTAD	-12.0	3.0	20.0	38.0	68.0	118.0	98.0	70.0	-

Notes:
Tanzania: UNCTAD data are used for 1990-1, before national records began. Privatisation data for 1992-5 have been added to FDI. Data for 1996-8 are preliminary, and include privatisation revenue with FDI component.
South Africa: Figures are converted to US dollars using the Financial Rand rate. Discrepancies with UNCTAD might be explained by the fact that UNCTAD uses the less concessional Commercial Rand rate.

Sources:
All countries: UNCTAD, World Investment Report 1998, Annex Table B1 (for 1992-7); 1997 Table B1 (for 1991), and 1996 Annex Table 1 (for 1990).
South Africa: South African Reserve Bank.
Tanzania: Bank of Tanzania; National Bank of Commerce; Parastatal Sector Reform Commission.
Uganda: Macro Policy Department, MEFP.
Zambia: Bank of Zambia.
Zimbabwe: Reserve Bank of Zimbabwe.

Both UNCTAD and national data for our project countries indicate that the target countries of FDI are diversifying. They show larger flows to South Africa, Zambia and Zimbabwe — and dramatic increases for all countries (Table 1.2; Figs 1.5a-b). Most strikingly, FDI flows are most important and fastest growing for the least developed countries — Tanzania, Uganda and Zambia (Figure 1.5a). All three countries now have FDI inflow/GDP ratios well above the SSA average (Figure 1.6). Other least developed countries such as Ghana and Mali have also seen rapid rises from low starting points in the 1990s. As discussed in section 1.3.1 below, some of these increases are being misrecorded as residual balance of payments items.

FDI is coming from new source countries. During the 1990s there was remarkable diversification, as also experienced by many other developing countries. A wider range of European countries (notably Belgium, Germany and Italy) increased FDI, joining the traditionally dominant UK and France. However, in contrast to other developing regions, the US share of investment has declined and Japan's remains tiny except in Liberia.

Instead, most of the diversification has been due to new sources, notably South Africa, East Asian countries, and returning former residents. South Africa has been expanding rapidly into Africa since 1993 (though some of this is hidden in international statistics because South African company headquarters are nominally registered elsewhere). There have also been significant flows from neighbouring states into South Africa. China, Malaysia, Hong Kong, Taiwan and South Korea also became significant players before the Asian crisis, notably in construction and communications, with flows rising from virtually nil to an average of $160 million a year during 1994-95. Formerly resident Asians have returned huge amounts of private capital to Eastern and Southern Africa; though often previously classified as private transfers in the balance of payments, our country studies of Tanzania and Uganda found that 70-80% of these flows represent FDI (Kasekende *et al*, 1997; Kimei *et al*, 1997).

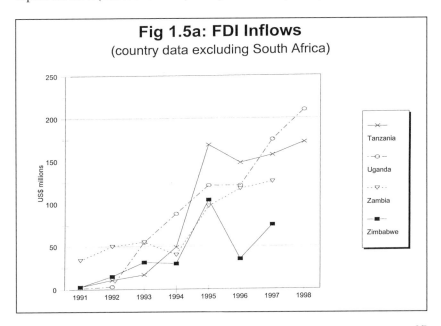

Fig 1.5a: FDI Inflows
(country data excluding South Africa)

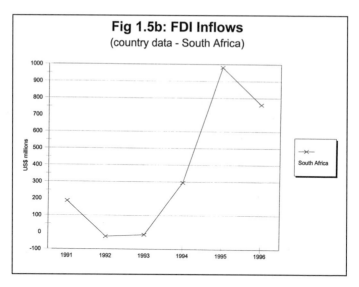

Fig 1.5b: FDI Inflows
(country data - South Africa)

At a country level, Zimbabwean national data show a dramatic shift in investment approvals, away from traditional OECD sources. Malaysia was the third largest source of FDI in 1996. China has invested strongly in construction, textiles and mining. Germany has become a major player via venture capital funds. On the other hand, UK and US investment has declined but, as with other large existing investors, their flows are under-stated in approvals due to the omission of reinvestment and new investment flows from parent firms.

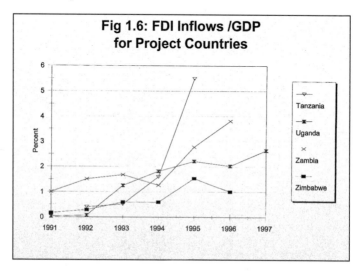

Fig 1.6: FDI Inflows /GDP for Project Countries

Finally, national data also show that FDI is diversifying out of petroleum and mining and into new sectors including agriculture, breweries and light manufacturing in Uganda, Tanzania, Zambia and Zimbabwe. International statistics are not tracking this because the absolute amounts continue to be dominated by a few large mining and oil projects, and because until recently smaller projects (especially those funded by "private transfers") have not been fully recorded by national databases.

1.2.2 Portfolio Equity

The major international data sources (World Bank and IMF) agree that portfolio equity is the fastest rising flow to SSA, from a very low base. However, while the World Bank shows it as the largest source of private capital in 1995 (Table 1.1), IMF data are much lower.

South Africa dominates the continent: inflows have risen sharply since 1992 and it receives more than 90% of total SSA flows. As a result, portfolio flows dominate total private flows to South Africa. International data also capture inflows for Zimbabwe, although before 1994 failed to capture this information, and after 1994 flows (excepting 1996) are underestimated in comparison with country data. There are no internationally recorded flows to Tanzania, Uganda or Zambia, although for Zambia flows measured through the Lusaka Stock Exchange (LUSE) have been quite significant since 1995 (Table 1.3).

However, beyond this broad picture, international data appear to be highly inaccurate. They are omitting large proportions of flows by failing to keep up with the liberalisation of financial markets globally and in Africa.

First, they are failing to reflect data from stock exchanges in Zambia and Zimbabwe on foreign participation in primary and secondary markets. The Lusaka Stock Exchange has reported flows for 1996-98 but international data show none. The Zimbabwe Stock Exchange reports much higher inflows and sharper rises for 1990-97 than international data.

Second, they are dramatically underestimating inflows through equity funds. Data from market sources, compiled especially for this study, reveal that South Africa, Zambia and Zimbabwe among other SSA countries have been receiving significant amounts via equity funds. Table 1.4 shows the main funds with SSA exposure. There are three types: "Pan-African" funds, South Africa-dedicated funds, and emerging market or global funds with some SSA exposure. Though the SSA exposure of global funds is only estimated, market participants suggest that the estimates are conservative. The total SSA portfolio investment stock of $10.3-12.3bn reflects unprecedented interest by portfolio investors since 1995. This includes adjust-

Table 1.3 Portfolio Equity Inflows (1990-98)
(millions of dollars)

	1990	1991	1992	1993	1994	1995	1996	1997	1998
South Africa									
Country data	-243.8	-550.1	-407.8	672.3	173.0	1326.7	1222.9		
World Bank	-	-	-	-	219.0	4571.0	1759.0	1393.2	-
IMF	-	-849.0	-806.0	877.0	133.0	1342.0	1243.0		
Zambia									
Country data	-	-	-	-	0.0	1.4	2.4	1.43	0.82
World Bank	0.0	0.0	0.0	0.0	0.0	0.0	0.0	0.0	-
Zimbabwe									
Country data	-21.7	7.3	-9.4	-4.8	49.6	63.7	-3.3	22.4	
World Bank	0.0	0.0	0.0	0.0	50.0	18.3	17.0	10.2	
IMF	-	-	-	-	56.9	-	-	-	

Notes:
Tanzania and Uganda receive no portfolio equity inflows.
Zambia is not captured by the IMF.

Sources:
All countries: World Bank, *Global Development Finance 1999*, and *Global Development Finance 1998*; IMF, *Balance of Payments Statistics Yearbook*, 1997.
South Africa: SARB Statistics on stock exchange transactions, 12/98.
Zambia: (1995-6) Bank of Zambia, *Annual Report 1997*; (1997-8) Lusaka Stock Exchange, *Monthly News Flash*, December 1998.
Zimbabwe: Reserve Bank of Zimbabwe database.

ments for the fact that, as shown in Table 1.5, around 30% of "Africa Fund" assets are actually invested in North Africa, Canada, Ireland, the UK or the US.

South Africa, traditionally the main recipient, accounts for over $8bn of dedicated funds, $270m (38% of SSA share) of Pan-African funds (Table 1.5, Fig 1.7), and most of the global emerging market fund exposure. However, 1995-98 saw considerable diversification out of South Africa. Zimbabwe and Mauritius are also key recipients. Nine Pan-African funds now invest in 16 SSA countries, set to rise to 19 once the West Africa Growth Fund has been fully allocated. Diversification for a particular fund is shown by comparing South Africa's share of its investment portfolio with South Africa's 90% share of market capitalisation. On this basis all but two funds have deliberately diversified, as confirmed by policy changes by fund managers: for example, the Mauritius Fund, initially dedicated to one country, now allows 10% exposure in Zimbabwe and Kenya.

Table 1.4 SSA Funds, and Exposure to Some Global Funds (in millions of dollars)

Funds	Management Company	Size	Structure	Launch
TOTAL		10,250.52 to 12,250.52		
TOTAL (ex SA funds)		2,192.92 to 4,192.92		
1. Pan Africa Funds		**692.90**		
Africa Emerging Markets	Emerging Mkts Investors Corp	114.80	Open from 11/97	Nov 93
Africa Investments	Morgan Stanley	315.50	Closed	Feb 94
Calvert New Africa	Calvert Asset Management Group	9.20	Open	Apr 95
GT Africa A&B Share	LGT Management	11.10	Open	Nov 93
Mauritius	Lloyds & Mauritius Fund Mgt	25.60	Closed	Jan 93
Simba	Baring Asset Mgt	29.80	Closed	Jan 96
Southern Africa	Alliance Capital	125.20	Closed	Feb 94
Southern Africa Investors Ltd	Mercury / Sanlam	27.20	Closed	Dec 95
Undervalued Assets Africa	Regent	8.20	Closed	Mar 97
West Africa Growth	Framlington	26.44	Closed	May 96
2. South Africa Funds [1]		**8,057.60**		
	ABSA	218.12		
	African Harvest	7.34		
	Allan Gray	1.36		
	BOE	499.10		
	Brait	46.30		
	Commercial Union	10.81		
	Community Growth	123.39		
	Coronation	591.98		
	Fedsure	91.02		
	Fleming Martin	34.30		
	FNB	0.70		
	Franklin Templeton	13.40		
	Guardbank	480.75		
	Investec	864.54		
	Cubed Capital	11.14		
	Marriott	26.56		
	Metropolitan	108.58		
	Nedcorp	812.91		
	Norwich	187.91		
	Old Mutual	1,727.96		
	Prestasi	4.12		
	PSG	14.37		
	RMB	331.99		
	Frank Russell	63.02		
	Sage	492.92		
	Sanlam	815.98		
	Southern	84.88		
	Standard Bank	392.15		
3. Global & Emerging Market Funds - est. SSA exposure [2]		**1,500 to 3,500**		

Notes:
1 Many South African Fund Managers run several funds - they are aggregated by manager here.
2 Market participants estimate 4-10% of global emerging market funds are invested in SSA. This makes between $1.5-3.5 billion, out of an IMF estimated total of $36 billion. We have very limited disaggregated data for this category: Foreign & Colonial have SSA exposure of $160 million; Morgan Stanley $30 million, and Flemings $14.4 million (or 7% exposure of their $180 million emerging market fund in South Africa, and 1% in Zimbabwe).

Sources:
Shareholder reports; interview material; Micropal Emerging Market Fund Monitor.

Table 1.5 **Exposure of Pan Africa-dedicated Funds by Recipient Country (1)**   (in millions of dollars)

	TOTAL		Africa Emerging Markets (2) 03/97		Africa Investments (3) 09/30/97		GT Africa (4) 09/30/98		Mauritius 12/31/98	
	%	US$m	%	US$m	%	US$m	%	US$m	%	US$m
TOTAL FUNDS	**100.0**	**692.9**	**100.0**	**114.8**	**100.0**	**315.5**	**100.0**	**11.1**	**100.0**	**25.6**
SSA Invested	**69.8**	**484.7**	**59.3**	**67.9**	**71.7**	**226.3**	**70.8**	**7.9**	**100.0**	**25.6**
SSA Invested (ex SA)	35.1	244.2	59.3	67.9	37.6	118.5	49.1	5.4	100.0	25.6
Botswana	3.1	21.2	6.6	7.6	3.1	9.9	7.0	0.8	-	-
Ghana	2.6	18.1	3.3	3.8	3.7	11.8	9.3	1.0	-	-
Ivory Coast	0.6	4.4	1.0	1.1	0.5	1.4	-	-	-	-
Kenya	2.2	15.2	5.2	6.0	1.8	5.6	11.1	1.2	2.1	0.5
Malawi	0.2	0.8	-	-	-	-	2.0	0.2	-	-
Mali	0.0	0.1	-	-	-	-	-	-	-	-
Mauritania	0.0	0.1	0.1	0.1	-	-	-	-	-	-
Mauritius	9.7	67.4	11.8	13.5	7.6	24.0	5.9	0.7	97.9	25.1
Mozambique	0.0	0.2	-	-	-	-	1.5	0.2	-	-
Namibia	1.1	7.4	5.9	6.7	-	-	-	-	-	-
Niger	0.1	0.4	0.4	0.4	-	-	-	-	-	-
Senegal	0.4	3.0	0.1	0.1	-	-	-	-	-	-
South Africa	34.7	240.4	-	-	34.2	107.9	21.7	2.4	-	-
Swaziland	0.2	1.7	1.5	1.7	-	-	-	-	-	-
Zambia	1.6	11.2	3.6	4.2	1.7	5.5	7.6	0.8	-	-
Zimbabwe	13.2	91.5	18.4	21.1	19.1	60.2	4.7	0.5	-	-
Egypt	14.5	100.3	18.9	21.7	21.4	67.4	17.1	1.9	-	-
Morocco	3.7	25.8	15.5	17.8	2.2	7.0	8.9	1.0	-	-
Tunisia	0.1	0.9	0.8	0.9	-	-	-	-	-	-
Non-Africa	0.8	5.3	-	-	1.7	5.3	-	-	-	-
Others	2.2	15.1	1.4	1.7	3.0	9.4	-	-	-	-
Offshore mining	0.3	2.4	-	-	-	-	1.6	0.2	-	-
Multinationals	0.2	1.2	-	-	-	-	-	-	-	-
Short-term notes	0.1	0.5	-	-	-	-	-	-	-	-
Cash (uninvested)	7.1	49.2	5.7	6.5	-	-	1.0	0.1	-	-

Table 1.5 (continued)

	Simba 12/31/97		Southern Africa Investors Ltd. 10/30/98		Southern Africa 11/30/96		Undervalued Assets Africa 12/31/97		West Africa Growth (6) 02/05/99	
	%	US$m	%	US$m (5)	%	US$m	%	US$m	%	US$m
TOTAL FUNDS	**100.0**	**29.8**	**100.0**	**27.2**	**100.0**	**125.2**	**100.0**	**8.2**	**100.0**	**26.4**
SSA Invested	**53.0**	**15.8**	**40.5**	**11.0**	**99.6**	**124.7**	**31.1**	**2.6**	**11.0**	**2.9**
SSA Invested (ex SA)	**28.0**	**8.3**	**5.6**	**1.5**	**9.8**	**12.3**	**21.1**	**1.7**	**11.0**	**2.9**
Botswana	5.0	1.5	-	-	0.7	0.9	7.7	0.6	-	-
Ghana	3.0	0.9	0.5	0.1	-	-	5.2	0.4	-	-
Ivory Coast	6.0	1.8	-	-	-	-	-	-	-	-
Kenya	3.0	0.9	0.8	0.2	-	-	8.2	0.7	-	-
Malawi	-	-	2.2	0.6	-	-	-	-	-	-
Mali	-	-	0.4	0.1	-	-	-	-	-	-
Mauritania	-	-	-	-	-	-	-	-	-	-
Mauritius	8.0	2.4	-	-	1.4	1.8	-	-	-	-
Mozambique	-	-	-	-	-	-	-	-	-	-
Namibia	-	-	-	-	0.5	0.6	-	-	-	-
Niger	-	-	-	-	-	-	-	-	-	-
Senegal	-	-	-	-	-	-	-	-	11.0	2.9
South Africa	25.0	7.5	34.9	9.5	89.8	112.4	10.0	0.8	-	-
Swaziland	-	-	-	-	-	-	-	-	-	-
Zambia	-	-	0.2	0.1	0.5	0.6	-	-	-	-
Zimbabwe	3.0	0.9	1.5	0.4	6.7	8.4	-	-	-	-
Egypt	29.0	8.6	-	-	-	-	8.2	0.7	-	-
Morocco	-	-	-	-	-	-	-	-	-	-
Tunisia	-	-	-	-	-	-	-	-	-	-
Non-Africa	-	-	-	-	-	-	-	-	-	-
Others	6.0	1.8	-	-	-	-	27.2	2.2	-	-
Offshore mining	-	-	-	-	-	-	26.8	2.2	-	-
Multinationals	4.0	1.2	-	-	-	-	-	-	-	-
Short-term notes-	-	-	-	0.4	0.5	-	-	-	-	-
Cash (uninvested)	8.0	2.4	59.5	16.2	-	-	6.5	0.5	89.0	23.5

Notes:
1) excludes funds dedicated exclusively to South Africa. Total includes the US$9.8m Calvert New Africa Fund, for which no details were available.
2) "Others" is classified by the fund management as "Africa-Regional".
3) "Non-Africa" comprises investments in Ireland, the US and the UK.
4) "Others" means other SSA investments.
5) Total asset value converted into US$ at exchange rate of UK£1 = US$1.6588.
6) The first investment was placed in February 1998. It is expected that the bulk will be invested in the 6 "core" Francophone economies: Ivory Coast, Senegal, Congo, Cameroon, Gabon and Mali.

Sources:
Shareholder reports; interviews with fund managers; World Equity.

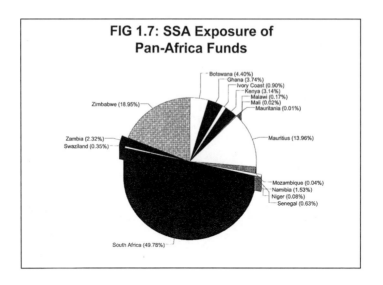

FIG 1.7: SSA Exposure of Pan-Africa Funds

Botswana (4.40%)
Ghana (3.74%)
Ivory Coast (0.90%)
Kenya (3.14%)
Malawi (0.17%)
Mali (0.02%)
Mauritania (0.01%)
Zimbabwe (18.95%)
Zambia (2.32%)
Swaziland (0.35%)
Mauritius (13.96%)
Mozambique (0.04%)
Namibia (1.53%)
Niger (0.08%)
Senegal (0.63%)
South Africa (49.78%)

1.2.3 Bank Loans

Due to different definitions and compilation methods, international data on bank flows agree only on the fact that the level of net inflows to SSA has been low (Table 1.1, Fig 1.8). The BIS and World Bank show volatile trends, though BIS sees a sharp rise since 1996. The IMF shows a positive trend to 1996.

On an annual basis, international data bear little relation to our country data (Table 1.6), but both agree that overall net bank flows have risen only for South Africa since 1993 and to a lesser extent for Tanzania (Figures 1.9a-b). Our country data indicate that they have remained highly volatile for Zambia and Zimbabwe, and negligible for Uganda.

However, it is vital to distinguish two groups of loans. Long-term bank loans are insignificant in all countries except South Africa, where they are rising. On the other hand, net short-term flows have been increasing and have exceeded long-term flows in all project countries except South Africa, where they remain volatile. Unguaranteed net flows have risen for all countries except Zambia over the 1990s (Table 1.7), with renewed interest in South Africa from 1994, Tanzania from 1996, and Zimbabwe from 1995.

Table 1.6 Net External Bank Flows for Project Countries (1990-97)
(millions of dollars)

	1990	1991	1992	1993	1994	1995	1996	1997
South Africa								
Country data	223.0	656.7	1,001.9	-1,998.3	384.5	3,544.0	2,274.0	-
BIS	-411.0	-844.0	27.0	-1,175.0	1,182.0	1,446.0	1,820.0	3,418.0
GDF	-	-	-	-	-245.6	-791.2	-1,478.3	-656.4
Tanzania								
Country data	5.9	8.4	13.7	24.2	42.6	75.9	27.9	58.8
BIS	-31.0	-54.0	2.0	-44.0	6.0	3.0	13.0	27.0
World Bank	0.0	-3.0	-7.0	-7.0	0.0	-4.0	-2.0	-
Uganda								
Country data	16.7	-9.2	0.8	-1.1	4.4	-11.5	-21.8	-0.1
BIS	11.0	-41.0	-6.0	112.0	-2.0	8.0	30.0	-20.0
World Bank	-10.0	-14.0	-3.0	-2.0	-6.0	-7.0	-6.0	-
Zambia								
Country data	-150.0	46.0	-40.0	35.7	-47.5	35.4	235.8	225.3
BIS	62.0	-43.0	-1.0	-80.0	-19.0	-87.0	28.0	-41.0
World Bank	2.0	5.0	10.0	-1.0	-1.0	6.0	0.0	-
Zimbabwe								
Country data	119.0	-1.6	360.6	-96.0	-251.4	137.2	-8.0	-80.0
BIS	152.0	359.0	54.0	-138.0	-81.0	148.0	35.0	190.0
World Bank	81.0	42.0	87.0	-70.0	-70.0	173.0	58.0	-

Sources:
World Bank, *Global Development Finance 1999*, data are medium and long-term only.
BIS data are for short term, and medium and long term.
South Africa data are converted to US$ using the less concessional Commercial Rand rate (whereas FDI and Portfolio data use the FinRand rate).
Tanzania CS-DRMS for "net flows" (MLT only). Short-term gross data added for 1994-5, as net not available.
Uganda (Table 9) - trade credits (net).
Zambia (Annex Table 1, p. 95) - short-term plus long-term loans (net).
Zimbabwe - short-term (net) plus long-term debt (net).

Table 1.7 Unguaranteed Net Bank Flows (1990-7)
(millions of dollars)

	1990	1991	1992	1993	1994	1995	1996	1997	Total
South Africa	-754	-1,129	-904	-1,281	1,337	2,521	2,118	2,997	**4,905**
Tanzania	-11	-1	-18	-6	3	-1	80	29	**75**
Uganda	12	-27	-19	132	-17	-3	27	-23	**82**
Zambia	71	-7	-3	-77	-15	44	-13	-37	**-37**
Zimbabwe	169	250	-113	-213	-95	208	53	167	**426**

Source:
Bank for International Settlements.

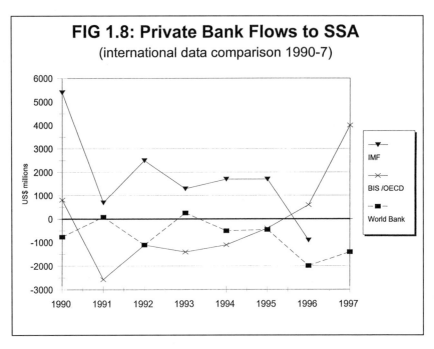

FIG 1.8: Private Bank Flows to SSA
(international data comparison 1990-7)

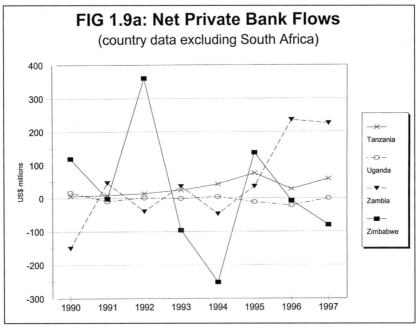

FIG 1.9a: Net Private Bank Flows
(country data excluding South Africa)

36

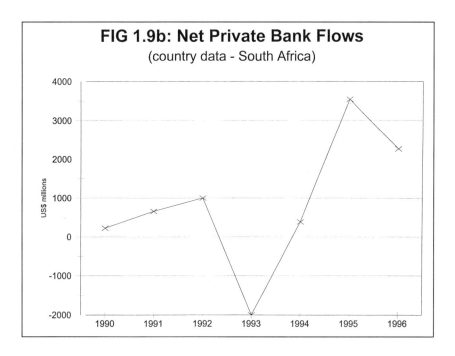

FIG 1.9b: Net Private Bank Flows
(country data - South Africa)

Tanzania, Uganda and Zambia also suggest that flows are substantially under-reported due to delays or omissions in data submitted by commercial to central banks. This is particularly true for short-term trade-related flows, which for example in Zambia are often classified in errors and omissions (Kasekende *et al* 1997; Kimei *et al*, 1997:2, 5-7; Matale *et al* 1997:13).

1.2.4 Bonds

Internationally issued bonds have been scarce, partly because few SSA countries have credit ratings high enough to make them creditworthy (see Chapter 5). Thus only four countries have issued bonds since 1994, South Africa accounting for the largest amount (Table 1.8). Again international data are inconsistent. World Bank data show the largest outflow from the region was in 1993 and inflow in 1994 (Table 1.1). This contrasts strongly with IMF data which show high net positive flows over the period, largely to South Africa, Nigeria and Namibia (Table 1.8). Although Congo issued bonds in 1994, the IMF records no associated flows. Data for foreign investor purchases and sales of domestically issued, domestic currency denominated South African government bonds provided by the South

African Reserve Bank, show this to be extremely volatile over the period, reaching a low in 1993, and peaking in 1995 (Table 1.9).

Table 1.8 International Bond Issues and Net Flows
(millions of dollars)

	1990	1991	1992	1993	1994	1995	1996
Issues							
SSA TOTAL	-	-	-	0	1,317	1,242	1,220
Congo	-	-	-	0	492	0	0
Ghana	-	-	-	0	0	0	250
Mauritius	-	-	-	0	0	150	0
South Africa	-	-	-	0	825	1,092	970
Flows (net)							
SSA TOTAL	-264	486	2,548	260	1,507	1,420	1,211
Côte d'Ivoire	-	-	-	-	-2	-	-
Mauritius	-	-	-	-	-	154	-
Namibia	15	-12	-	63	30	53	-10
Nigeria	-197	-61	1,884	-18	-27	-72	-151
Senegal	-	7	-	-	-	-	-
South Africa*	-50	586	700	221	1,514	1,293	1,459
Zimbabwe	-32	-35	-37	-5	-7	-	-

Note:
* IMF, *Balance of Payments Statistics Yearbook 1997* data for net flows to South Africa differ for 1994 and 1995 in Volume 1 (country tables), and Volume 2 by region. Volume 2 gives US$1999m and US$821m respectively. Volume 1 figures are used here as they are consistent with the SSA total in Table 1.1. Both years aggregate to roughly the same in either volume.

Source:
Issues from Euromoney Bondware and World Bank Staff estimates in World Bank *Global Development Finance* Vol.1, 1997, p.108, 111. Flows from IMF, Balance of Payments Statistics Yearbook 1997, Vol.1.

Table 1.9 Foreign Investor Purchases and Sales of Domestically Issued, Domestic Currency Denominated South African Government Bonds
(millions of dollars)

1990	1991	1992	1993	1994	1995	1996
500.9	801.7	776.1	104.8	1,330.5	2,235.7	1,782.0

Source: South African Reserve Bank.

1.3 Monitoring

The previous section of this chapter has amply demonstrated the existing flaws and inconsistencies in data on private capital flows to Africa. In turn these reflect flaws in the recording methods used by African governments and international institutions.

1.3.1 African Governments

Just when flows to the region have been increasing, many African governments have virtually abandoned monitoring. For many, monitoring sprang from comprehensive exchange control regimes. As they have liberalised their external sectors, monitoring has gradually been eroded, making it difficult to analyse trends in capital flows. As discussed in Section 1.2 above, this applies particularly to FDI, private transfers and bank loans, because investment centres, forex bureaux and banks are not monitoring flows in a timely or accurate fashion or reporting them to central banks.

Two additional factors have undermined monitoring of private flows: scepticism about the desirability of monitoring, due to concern that it may be perceived wrongly by investors as a step back to capital controls; and (given that scepticism) a reluctance to devote scarce government staff resources to the task.

The resulting major underestimates of private flows, and inconsistencies between international and country data sets, have had several important pernicious effects:

- most important, African goverments have been less able to formulate appropriate and stable macroeconomic policy, by understanding the causes, effects and sustainability of flows, and attracting desirable and stable flows. As a senior policymaker put it, "the difficulty in analysing policy response to the recent capital flows lies mainly in the absence of the relevant data and forecasts that could enable the authorities to react in a timely and consistent fashion" (Kimei *et al*, 1997:30).

- African and donor governments and international agencies such as the International Finance Corporation (IFC) and Commonwealth Development Corporation (CDC), which are responsible for promoting foreign private capital flows and the African private sector, have based their strategies on erroneous and underestimated data and have until recently tended to target the least dynamic sources of investment such as OECD multinationals, large banks and bond issuers, rather than dynamic African regional and developing country investors, equity funds and short-term trade finance;

- potential sources of international capital flows (investors, fund managers, bankers) have perceived Africa as receiving virtually no flows, and therefore been discouraged from investing more;
- those responsible for analysing creditworthiness (rating agencies, export credit agencies, central bank regulators) have continued to perceive high country risk and low government credibility, and therefore to discourage flows;
- in the absence of accurate data, African governments have been either excessively pessimistic or (more often) optimistic about prospects for access to private capital flows, thereby reducing their requests for public sector finance (aid and debt relief).

Ceasing to monitor in a climate of rapidly increasing flows is highly damaging and, as many Latin American and East Asian countries have shown, by liberalising capital accounts but retaining strict monitoring, the two can go together happily (Helleiner, 1997).

In the light of the scale and economic importance of private capital flows into Africa, governments, international organisations and donors now all acknowledge that top-quality, accurate and timely data are essential to policy formulation. Officials from African countries have repeatedly identified this as a priority for the region (EFA, 1997; EFA/MEFMI, 1997; MEFMI 1997). In response to these demands, EFA and CREFSA are now working with 6 African governments to build their capacity to monitor flows (Box 1.1).

The capital flows study and data monitoring workshop have revealed that governments throughout Africa have problems assessing the nature and magnitude of private capital flows. However, some have much more developed recording systems, and individual countries monitor some types of flow far better than others. In general, countries fall into two groups. The first has successful monitoring systems, but wishes to deepen or rationalise current practices to reach international standards such as the General Data Dissemination System and more advanced Special Data Dissemination Standard established by the International Monetary Fund. The second is introducing or reviving monitoring systems, lacks up-to-date time series and fails to record many elements (such as sources of funds for bureaux and bank customers).

Box 1.1 Capacity-Building in Monitoring Private Capital Flows

Six governments in Eastern and Southern Africa, with assistance from EFA and CREFSA and funding from the Swedish, Danish and British governments, are working to improve their monitoring and analysis of private capital flows, to match the international standards of bodies such as the IMF and OECD. This began with a workshop on recording private capital flows in Pretoria in July 1998, to recommend improvements based on regional and international best practices. It shared regional and international best practices on technical and institutional issues, and developed country-specific strategies to improve data quality. It was attended by high-level officials and technical experts from central banks, investment centres, and stock and bond exchanges from 14 countries (Botswana, Ghana, Kenya, Lesotho, Malawi, Mauritius, Mozambique, Namibia, South Africa, Swaziland, Tanzania, Uganda, Zambia, and Zimbabwe), and by experts from the Bank of England, the International Monetary Fund, the National Bank of Belgium and the National Bank of Poland. Plenary sessions were devoted to FDI, portfolio investment, bank and private-sector debt flows, and foreign exchange bureau flows, cash transactions and residual flows; each included international and regional presentations. Countries then split into working groups to develop country-specific data strategies, comprising a plan of action for methodological and institutional improvements.

EFA and CREFSA are continuing to meet the capacity-building needs of African countries by supporting intra-regional cooperation on capacity-building and research. Teams of government officials in Mozambique, South Africa, Tanzania, Uganda, Zambia and Zimbabwe are conducting a study examining intra-regional private capital flows in Eastern and Southern Africa, in which the SADC Finance and Investment Sector Coordinating Unit (based in the South African Department of Finance) is playing a leading role. The study will allow policymakers to identify how to encourage regional flows (which tend to be more sustainable) by analysing their scale and economic importance, relative sustainability, sectoral distribution, and determinants of investment decisions. The project is also building regional capacity to monitor and measure flows and to design appropriate policy responses, by developing innovative survey and analysis methodologies. Findings were presented at a workshop in June 1999, and will be published shortly.

All countries share the following problems:

- huge unidentified private capital flows, which appear in residual categories, and seem to hide FDI data. In South Africa, "unrecorded transactions" reached 2.6% of GDP in 1993, equalling identified flows (Khatri *et al*, 1997). In Tanzania, "private transfers" reached 39% of flows in 1995. The Investment Promotion Centre (IPC) does not record approvals below $0.5m, or FDI ineligible for its incentives. Most private transfers are residents or non-residents returning capital for investment in small businesses or construction (Kimei *et al*, 1997:1-8). In Uganda, "private transfers" have exceeded 4% of GDP for the last decade, reaching 76% of private flows in 1995. They come through bureaux and banks, which classify all remittances as transfers when they cannot identify their purpose. Much of this is FDI by returning Asian Ugandans (Kasekende *et al*, 1997:11, Sajjabi *et al*, 1998:6-7). In Zambia, "errors and omissions" have been consistently high and negative, exceeding recorded flows until 1993. They have grown with bureaux and foreign currency accounts, and liberalisation of the capital account. They reflect capital flight, small-scale FDI and short-term debt (Matale *et al*, 1997:13). In Zimbabwe, improvements in recording have reduced "errors and omissions" from 25% of flows in 1985-90, by identifying them as FDI and portfolio investment (Kufeni *et al*, 1997:14).
- problems distinguishing private and official flows, due to increasing interaction between official institutions and the private sector. For example, how should countries treat investments by the IFC or the CDC in stock markets, or other private ventures?
- uncertainty in classifying the "term" (long or short) of flows, because some flows traditionally classified as "long-term" have proved highly volatile. For example, bonds and bank loans can increasingly be sold in secondary markets, indicating that there are no longer any true long-term capital flows.
- weaknesses in the timeliness and periodicity of recorded data. Infrequent reporting or mismatches between the reporting periods for different types of flows make it impossible to assess their level and composition. For example, Bank of Tanzania's medium and long-term debt data are incomplete due to "a considerable reporting lag", although borrowers have to obtain prior approval from BOT (Kimei *et al*, 1997:1-6).

What causes the problems? The main factor is private sector non-compliance with reporting requirements, due to suspicion of the authorities, or failure to take form-filling seriously. This is exacerbated by non-existent or inadequate legal frameworks to enforce compliance (e.g. Zambia's Central Statistical Office in Matale *et al*, 1997:11), or to failure to enforce existing compliance mechanisms as in Uganda (Kasekende *et al*, 1997:10-11). The cause and result is "public apathy to documentation", due often to the pervasive nature of the black market. The problem is worsened by caution on the part of agencies executing transactions (commercial banks and bureaux), resulting from the fear that enforcement would "scare their customers", forcing them back into the black market (Kimei *et al*, 1997). Another disincentive is the proliferation of surveys by governmental, academic, and private bodies, duplicating the same questions, and without coordination.

However, it is remarkable that compliance varies by country and by type of flow. For example, Uganda's central bank and Investment Promotion Centre have experienced more problems on FDI than in Tanzania, but Bank of Uganda has better relations with forex bureaux than Bank of Tanzania. The key lesson is that there is no type of flow which cannot be recorded if governments are prepared to work at building relations with the protagonists.

Lack of cooperation among government agencies can cause gaps or double counting, and wastes resources by duplicating effort or assigning monitoring responsibility to agencies which have no connection with those executing transactions, or have inadequate human and financial resources. Tanzania's experience shows that cooperation among agencies with similar agendas, such as central banks and investment centres, can work wonders.

There are many regional "success stories" on which to build intra-regional cooperation on improving data quality, as shown in Box 1.2.

Box 1.2 Regional Success Stories

Many African governments are meeting or exceeding international best practices. South Africa, Botswana and Namibia have reached international standards on balance of payments (BOP) statistics by conducting integrated surveys.

FDI: Bank of Namibia
In 1990, Bank of Namibia created a BOP division in its research department to gather and analyse external sector data. It assembled a 12,000-entry database of businesses in a year, from which it ran two surveys. The first covered foreign assets/liabilities and trade, and the second focussed on BOP transactions. Initial problems of terminology, language, newness (some assumed Bank of Namibia was a commercial bank!), and confidentiality were overcome by simultaneous training and purchase of computer technology, learning lessons from the mistakes

---

of others, and help from a resident IMF advisor. Bank of Namibia now conducts targeted annual surveys and research studies of key sectors and topical issues, and works closely with other government departments. It has outstripped most countries in implementing the 5th edition of the IMF *Balance of Payments Manual* by 1997 (Scheun, 1998).

Portfolio Equity: Mauritius Stock Exchange Commission

The Mauritius Stock Exchange has grown rapidly since inception in 1989 in terms of capitalisation, turnover, and number of companies. It now lists 47 companies in tourism, banking, commerce, manufacturing, and sugar. Though the market was closed to foreigners until 1994, listing, auditing, accounting and trade recording now match international norms, thanks in large part to a computerised Central Depository and Settlement System (Dindoyal, 1998).

Bank Flows: Reserve Bank of Zimbabwe

The Reserve Bank of Zimbabwe recognised the need for multiple databases during liberalisation. RBZ's "EPIC" computer system, monitoring interbank foreign exchange transactions by a direct link to authorised dealers, has become essential as exchange controls have disappeared. EPIC captures exports and imports on a cash basis, service receipts and payments, income receipts and payments, cash transfers, and cash capital flows including pre/post shipment finance, portfolio investment, and external debt payments. The UNCTAD DMFAS system captures foreign exchange transactions such as short and medium to long-term loans used for purchasing equipment offshore. It is therefore relatively straightforward to combine the findings of both databases into reports, with the advantage that there is no danger of double counting (Kufeni *et al*, 1997:37-8, Mkwebu and Mpofu, 1998).

Foreign Exchange Flows (Bureaux and Commercial Banks): Bank of Uganda

Uganda receives significant inflows of foreign exchange in the form of "private transfers". As a result, Bank of Uganda has taken steps to identify these flows through a system of surveys, focussing on the source and purpose of such flows. It has successfully sensitised banks and bureaux to the necessity of reporting, by stressing the benefits they can obtain from more comprehensive market information. Compliance with these surveys has therefore been high, enabling Bank of Uganda to draw strong conclusions on the nature of these flows (see Sajjabi and Ddamulira, 1998).

1.3.2 International Organisations

Data produced by the international organisations generally come from national sources, but their quality in terms of disaggregation, timeliness or period coverage varies dramatically.

FDI data are generally the most disaggregated and complete. UNCTAD data are the best, because they fill gaps in the "reliable and comprehensive" IMF *Balance of Payments Statistics Yearbook* (BOPSY) with data from recipient countries and the OECD. However, they suffer from 1-2 year lags in national reporting, and unreliable preliminary data, which lead to major underestimates and later upward revisions — and from the omission from national statistics of elements such as reinvested earnings and intra-company loans. UNCTAD also often has inadequate resources to quality control national data, for example with accurate ratios of the historical amount of FDI inflows compared to approvals (which may vary from 20-60%).

Portfolio investment data inconsistencies reflect the newness of these flows. The result is confusion in identification in recipient countries, which feeds through to international data sets, leading to dramatic revisions of data (e.g. the World Bank's preliminary 1995 data of $0.5bn shot up to $5bn (World Bank 1996 and 1997b). While World Bank data are generally the most comprehensive in their country coverage and because they tap recipient and market sources, all compilers agree that there is no adequate global database.

Data on bank flows are hampered by the absence of a single comprehensive database. World Bank data do not separate private from publicly guaranteed short-term flows, though they have the advantage of supplementing debtor with creditor sources drawn from the OECD. BIS data cover short-term debt but are restricted to banks reporting from within the BIS area and come from creditor sources. The most reliable databases on bonds are in the private sector, though the World Bank tracks all of these: but inconsistent recording mechanisms make international data highly variable.

International organisations have faithfully reported the residual unrecorded flows (IMF) or omitted them from their report on capital flows (UNCTAD; World Bank). Though some technical assistance missions have recommended steps to improve recording, they have usually failed to provide the strategies for building permanent capacity and a culture of reporting which are essential to sustainable monitoring. Botswana and Namibia are rare success stories where they have provided sustained assistance.

In the context of the crises in capital flows in the mid-1990s, international organisations have repeatedly exhorted countries to improve their monitoring of flows. They have held international conferences and seminars on recording and dissemination standards. Yet, as at mid-1999, there exists no comprehensive programme by any international organisation to assist countries on the ground to build their capacity to monitor and analyse private capital flows, by supporting them in introducing surveys and analytical techniques. Indeed it would be fair to say that African governments (with some external assistance) have made far greater efforts than the international financial institutions to improve their monitoring.

1.4 Conclusion

Private capital flows to SSA have been much greater than previously believed, and their growth and economic importance match those of other developing regions. FDI is diversifying its source and recipient countries and sectors, largely due to innovation by non-OECD investors. Portfolio flows are rising the fastest, with the creation of new stock exchanges and international equity funds, which are diversifying beyond South Africa. Bank flows and bonds have stagnated, though country data show short-term loans rising.

Data on the flows remain poor. African governments are only just beginning to reverse their earlier decisions to abandon monitoring (prompted by worries about the credibility of liberalisation and underestimates of the costs of poor monitoring — which were in turn often inspired by external organisations). They continue to face severe monitoring problems in spite of some donor assistance. Although there are many regional success stories on which to build intra-regional cooperation in improving data, governments continue to face a lack of will to report by the private sector, and inadequate cooperation among government agencies. Data sets of international organisations build on (and therefore magnify) these flaws. Poor data have undermined macroeconomic policy, decisions by donors, investors and credit analysts, and flows of aid and debt relief, as discussed in the following chapters.

Part 2

Perception and the Causes of Flows

Chapter 2 Foreign Direct Investment

Nils Bhinda, Stephany Griffith-Jones and Matthew Martin

2.1 Introduction

Chapter 1 showed that, contrary to widely held opinion, FDI to many Sub-Saharan African countries has increased rapidly in the 1990s. It remains the most important flow absolutely, and is larger relative to many African countries' GDP than in most other developing countries. Yet flows have risen more slowly than some countries have turned around their economies and established political stability. Why?

Many factors influencing FDI apply to other flows. Most important is lack of information. The information which flows to investors is often inaccurate and out of date. Major investment promotion campaigns fail to overcome distortions and exaggerations in a sensationalist international press. Most international investors cite negative press as powerfully discouraging investment. Even successful countries suffer from negative information about the continent as a whole: "potential investors lump them together with other countries, as part of a continent that is considered not to be attractive" (UNCTAD, 1995b). This is a mirror image of the euphoria about all East Asian markets before the 1997 currency crises. The underlying problem is the short memory and copy-cat behaviour of many Western investors, while regionally-based investors, who are better-informed and less prejudiced, are investing widely and reaping the rewards.

But FDI is different in one major respect: it is difficult to reverse and to a degree irreversible. This generates caution in three ways. First, investors adopt a "wait-and-see" attitude. This creates a vicious circle. If caution reduces investment in a given year, the resulting decline in productive capacity then fulfils their negative expectations, resulting in a low investment equilibrium (ADB, 1993:173). Second, many investors favour a shorter investment time horizon: "the basic rule for black Africa is to get your money back as soon as possible, or don't do it. Who knows what's going to happen next year?". As a result, many foreign investors borrow from local financial institutions, using real assets as security, and repatriate their initial investment immediately. The exceptions are mining companies and plantations, which make such high returns that they are prepared to be involved longer-term.

The rest of this chapter examines in more detail the national and sectoral causes of FDI. These are closely interlinked: once a country achieves political stability and economic growth, investors focus on sectoral factors.

2.2 Causes Related to Source Countries

As shown in Chapter 1, the source countries of FDI in Africa are changing dramatically in the 1990s. While "traditional" Western investors still account for the bulk of stock and flows, new links are being established with the Far East. The most striking recent development is the growth of a regional market, which is provoking huge intra-regional investments, notably by South African companies and returning South Asian investors.

2.2.1 South Africa

South Africa has become a potent regional influence since its peaceful transition to democracy. Its proximity, sophistication and market size give it strong natural comparative advantages to take a leading role in the region. Since 1995, South African investors have blazed a trail into the region, beginning in high-profit sectors such as breweries, retailing, financial services, mining and tourism, but more recently diversifying into agriculture and manufacturing. They have been encouraged by South Africa's selective liberalisation of capital controls, which has given preference to investment in the region.

2.2.2 Asian Business Groups

Outside South Africa, the most dynamic regional investors have been the Asian community. Much of their returned capital is hidden in "private transfers", concealing the FDI purpose revealed by interviews with Asian business people in the UK and Africa. Their motivations have until now been ill-understood, but they have been strongly influenced by the changed attitudes to their communities of national political leaders. This has been most remarkable in Uganda, which has successfully targeted dispossessed groups to return, using incentives and well planned investment promotion missions led by the President himself. Many of the regional business "empires" have their roots in the Ugandan Asian community.

Of course, there is great diversity within the "Asian community". Tanzania provides a striking example: the Muslims are divided into Shias, Ismailis and Khojas, and non-Muslims include Hindus, Parsees and Sikhs. Not surprisingly, "cultural divisions within the Asian minority are at least as large as those between Asian and African Tanzanians" (Lofchie and Callaghy, 1995:48). But most African officials and donors tend not to differentiate among these groups, showing alarming ignorance. The interactions within and among these communities deserve more study.

2.2.3 The Far East

Until 1997, and especially after 1994-95, interest from Far Eastern companies was growing rapidly, with major increases from China, Malaysia, Hong Kong, Taiwan and South Korea. South Africa was the main initial destination, but during 1995-97 investors increasingly diversified into Botswana, Ghana, the Seychelles, Tanzania, Uganda and Zimbabwe. In contrast, Japan's involvement remains limited. Investors are discouraged by the absence of Japanese trading companies, banks and External Trade Organisation offices, and weak trade relations (only 1.2% of Japanese exports go to Africa). Africa receives 10% of Japan's ODA, but this is largely for humanitarian and social sector projects rather than public-private partnership loans for infrastructure, and so has not stimulated FDI (UNCTAD, 1996:48-50). Nevertheless, most of these obstacles have been overcome or ignored by investors from other Asian countries, which rely less on these types of "developed country" financial patterns and support institutions. Unfortunately for Africa, as the "final frontier" for Asian investment, it has suffered even more than other regions from a cut in Asian overseas investment in 1997-9 due to the economic crisis.

2.2.4 Western Europe and the US

While FDI sources are diversifying, most still comes from the UK and France, reflecting colonial ties. The French are largely in the CFA Zone, and the UK in Anglophone Africa, mainly Kenya, Nigeria, and Zimbabwe. Their flows have increased since the first half of the 1980s when some manufacturers pulled out from politically and economically unstable areas (Bennell, 1995). Nevertheless, these investors are among the least expansionary in the region: their long experience of the region has tended to breed a degree of complacency. Relatively few new Western investors have been coming to Africa outside South Africa — they are the most subject to the perception of black Africa as a basket case area. Yet data for US affiliates in Africa show the return on FDI has been far higher than in Latin America, and above both developed and developing country averages (UNCTAD, 1997a:60-1),

2.2.5 Contrasting Psychological Attitudes

Perhaps the weakest reason for not investing, but one of the most pervasive influences on actual investment, is the diversity of psychological attitudes among different source countries. Japanese tend to feel "cultures do not fit together", but many other Far Eastern, Asian and South African investors have overcome similar distance. In the same way, UK companies suggest that, owing to ties going back over generations, East African Asians are "closer to the ground" in a way the British may once have been, and therefore more attuned to the business culture. It is difficult to escape the conclusion that the potential OECD investor does not want to solve this problem. As a UK Asian investor in East Africa said, "an aloof attitude lets the British investor down".

One additional important factor is the lack of a "strategic" motivation for investing in Africa. Geopolitical factors play a large role in US investment in Latin America, Japanese involvement in Asia and European flows to Central and Eastern Europe and North Africa. In spite of major efforts by the African-American community and the current US government, there is no similar strategic interest in Africa by any developed country.

2.3 Structural Factors

2.3.1 Market Size

Inadequate individual national markets are an important deterrent for many OECD (notably Japanese) firms which intend to service the domestic market. The three main components are low income (GDP per capita) which reduces purchases of high-cost goods, a resulting low domestic savings rate which limits local investment, and a small domestic market (measured in GDP or population) which makes information costs high relative to potential sales, reducing margins and limiting expansion. The exceptions have been South Africa, Nigeria, Zimbabwe and the middle-income Francophone countries.

However, dynamic investors have developed three alternative strategies. Some focus on low-cost goods (as one investor expressed it, "there are some goods everybody has to use"). Others (notably Far Eastern, Asian community and South African firms) aim explicitly for the higher-income South African market: for example, Malaysia is investing in Botswana to produce for South Africa. A third group focuses only on exports outside the region.

The regional market is therefore vital to many firms' "critical mass". Investors have been made more optimistic by regional trade liberalisation through COMESA, the East African Community and the Cross-Border Initiative. But the benefits appear to be concentrated in the economically stronger states (as forecast by Riddell and Cockcroft, 1991:146). Smaller countries are suffering as businesses relocate to South Africa, which provides a better national income base and economies of scale on which to build a strategy for the regional market. Until 1998, similar factors were also encouraging investment in Zimbabwe, although to a lesser degree. The growth of oligopolistic regional business groups of South African, Zimbabwean and Asian companies is being encouraged by their easier access to trade finance and other credit, building on sound corporate financial positions and close links with international or Asian regional banks. Access to South African goods has brought major cost savings to Zambia, Tanzania, Uganda and Mozambique. However, transforming trade liberalisation into sustained development throughout the region will depend on closer cooperation in improving infrastructure and labour skills in the poorer countries — and on continued growth in South Africa to act as a magnet for global FDI.

2.3.2 Infrastructure

Poor infrastructure is cited as a minor disincentive by potential (especially OECD) investors. They use it as a catch-all term to cover almost any practical problem, including unreliable and expensive phone lines, power cuts, water shortages, and congested roads, rail or ports. However, existing investors and those based in the region — those who are having to cope with the problem — seem prepared to "make the best of the situation", and to acknowledge that most countries have made dramatic efficiency-enhancing improvements in the 1990s (in roads, power and notably telephones, due to widespread use of mobile phones and the internet, and the extension of regular phone lines), and that some countries — South Africa, Zambia, Zimbabwe and increasingly Uganda — have relatively few problems.

Financial infrastructure is also vital, and South Africa's developed banking system, akin to many first world countries, enables it to attract significant FDI (Riddell and Cockcroft, 1991). Zimbabwe also has had until recently a relatively strong and well developed financial sector. In contrast, in the country surveys conducted for this project, either actual or perceived potential problems mobilising local banking, leasing or equity finance, or conducting local financial operations through poor payments systems, were near the top of the list of factors discouraging investors in Tanzania,

Uganda and Zambia. High domestic interest rates due to inflation, inefficient local financial intermediation (and to the effects of capital inflows themselves!) were also a strong deterrent. To the degree that financial sector problems or underdevelopment deter local investment, they also deter foreign investors by indicating a low local investor confidence.

2.3.3 Labour

Low labour productivity hinders UK and Japanese FDI, with investors finding labour in other regions (especially Asia) to be better value. This concern is legitimate insofar as it focuses on low skills, which outweigh cheap wages, and spring in turn from poor education, and lack of on-the-job training and middle or senior level entrepreneurial experience. Again the picture varies from country to country, with Zimbabwean and South African workers more skilled and experienced than their Tanzanian and Zambian counterparts (see Kufeni et al, 1997:46). Yet in-country studies show dramatic recent improvements in productivity.

Another factor perceived by OECD investors as reducing productivity in South Africa is strong trade unionism due to labour legislation. Yet investors in Southern Africa felt that unions throughout the region were becoming more conciliatory, and were not a problem.

In this light, many (particularly UK and South African) companies employ expatriate managers to overcome skills gaps. Expatriates employed by UK companies in Africa actually increased between 1989 and 1993. According to interviewees, this reflected a need for more intensive management in a deteriorating business environment, and the out-migration of local managers. However, there is little evidence that expatriates have been replaced in countries experiencing economic recovery, even though they cost more than local staff. Probably the most powerful factor behind expatriate employment has been the liberalisation of legislative restrictions — though it can take time for legal changes to reach the field (in Zimbabwe, "the amount of time it takes for an investor, local or foreign, to get application papers processed to operate here is still too long" — Kufeni et al, 1997:29-30). Many acknowledged that the necessity for expatriates varies by country and sector; they employ local managers in South Africa and Zimbabwe, but expatriates in Tanzania and Zambia. Employing expatriates often causes resentment in the workforce — particularly against managers from other African countries. Yet few companies have a long-term timetabled plan for transferring responsibility to local managers, except if this is mandated under affirmative action programme in South Africa or Zimbabwe. One notable exception is the Mozal project in Mozambique.

Unfortunately, what often underlies investor perception and permanent employment of expatriates is the incorrect view that low productivity reflects immutable "cultural factors", sometimes manifested as primitive racism. A UK-based manufacturer of machetes and hoes with long involvement in Africa was singularly honest: "Africans are perfectly happy falling asleep under a mango tree and leading a subsistence life".

2.4 Economic Performance and Policy Factors

2.4.1 Economic Performance

Actual and perceived performance influence all investors. Among the least informed, notably the Japanese investors (UNCTAD, 1996), it takes the form of an inability to distinguish among countries, and a tendency to attribute negative performance to the whole region. Those closer to the ground easily find countries with strong economic fundamentals to encourage investment.

In view of the differing nature of structural adjustment programmes (SAPs), this study has eschewed simplistic tests of correlation between FDI and adjustment programmes, for which earlier studies have found mixed results. Though investors see the existence of a programme with the IMF or World Bank as a sign of stability and intent to reform, they do not rank this as an important factor in the investment decision. We have therefore preferred to join foreign investors in judging adjustment programmes by the effects of individual policies. However, investors note that some adjustment policies have helped (privatisation, trade reform, new investment codes, decontrol of forex and prices), but SAPs have neglected infrastructure, labour skills, and regional integration. They also stress that programmes need to be more tailored to complexity of local economies and to consult the private sector more directly in their design (see also Bennell, 1995:210). Where major investors perceive SAPs to have a negative effect or to be ignoring their interests, they often try to directly influence government policy in a different direction, in order to encourage inward investment. Many companies have lobbied for tariff or tax structures or labour laws favourable to their activities.

More important, investors are highly sensitive to reform credibility, and consistent and transparent execution. Credibility is fragile: "international experience has demonstrated that credibility may be lost overnight, but is only regained very slowly" (ADB, 1993:173). Investors therefore complain that programmes are too inflexible to cope with sudden economic shocks or regional problems, and that shocks, bad design or overhasty implementation can shatter credibility.

2.4.2 Foreign Exchange Availability

Potential foreign exchange shortages, risking delays or restrictions on remittances, are a major fear — because investors know that Africa remains highly vulnerable to aid shortfalls, terms of trade shocks, and the debt overhang. So are falling exchange rates, which reduce rates of return to parent companies (the main reason for UK disinvestment from SSA in the 1980s and early 1990s) and make imported inputs more expensive, though they favour exporters. One major company said that "impossibly high margins" were needed to survive the slide of the South African rand. This has since pushed his head office to invest elsewhere — although it would have been easy to hedge rand exposure in the deep South African markets.

Perception here is particularly far from reality. Even in days of foreign exchange shortages (in 1985-90) rates of return improved in many sectors, leaving the share of net earnings remitted each year from UK manufacturing investments in Africa well above the global average (Bennell, 1995). Yet even now, when forex restrictions have been lifted in most African countries, and though investors and analysis suggest this encourages higher investment (in Kenya, Tanzania, Uganda, Zambia and Zimbabwe), devaluation and restrictions remain at the back of investors' minds. As a result, while many publicly favour rapid removal of controls, they privately sympathise with a gradual approach (for example in South Africa).

2.4.3 Fiscal Policy

Fiscal policy, specifically tax levels, structure and coverage, are important for all investors. They want a simple, transparent and comprehensive tax system. Until the mid-1990s, many countries had so many taxes and levels that even investors with the best intentions to pay were not aware of them all. Meanwhile tax collection was minimal and evasion easy.

Investors appreciate efforts in the 1990s to streamline the tax structure by introducing VAT, and to improve tax collection through independent revenue authorities in South Africa, Tanzania, Uganda and Zambia (though these have not always been successful — see Chapter 7). Nevertheless, donor pressure on government to raise budget revenue, and the complexity of taxing the rural and informal sectors, have continued to force new taxes on the small formal sector. In Tanzania this is complicated by retroactive imposition of some taxes, and the feeling among investors that they are being taxed at least twice for the same thing with poor compliance and easy evasion. Many investors also feel strongly that government needs to increase spending on infrastructure and education/health to support private sector development. Overall, most therefore feel that fiscal policy is too tight.

Import duties can also work in many ways to influence investment, depending on the relative balance of imports and exports in the investor's potential business. High tariffs are often perceived as an extra cost (to be avoided where possible by getting duty exemptions or lobbying for tariff reductions), particularly where the FDI is import-dependent. They also are blamed for retaliatory tariff measures by other countries which undermine export-oriented investment. As for low tariffs, many investors in Zambia, whether producing for the domestic, regional or international market, felt that its degree of liberalisation (both in reducing tariffs on imports and in reducing subsidies or incentives for exports) put them at a competitive disadvantage compared to larger regional trading partners. Similarly, the degree of import penetration in a given sector in Zimbabwe was a strong disincentive to FDI. Overall, high tariffs can provide an incentive to invest behind a tariff wall — or can discourage investment — depending on import dependence.

2.4.4 Privatisation

Privatisation programmes have often been an entry point for FDI to a country or sector, and are perceived by investors to have had positive effects in Tanzania, Uganda, Zambia, Zimbabwe and South Africa. SSA sales of state owned enterprises (SOEs) were below the developing world average until 1995, with some notable exceptions such as Ghana's Ashanti Goldfields (1994), which brought large net inflows of foreign exchange (Table 2.1). However, 1995 saw a broadening of the countries in which sales were occurring, and 1996 a dramatic increase in gross privatisation revenue (though most of this reflected three large sales in Ghana, Kenya and South Africa).

Privatisation revenue as a source of FDI to SSA is important relative to other developing areas. It comprised 20% of total FDI in 1988-95 (Figure 2.1). This indicates high dependence on privatisation as a source of FDI: one third of Tanzanian and Ugandan recorded FDI since 1992-93 has come from privatisations (though this is well above the SSA average). World Bank data show that FDI was 42% of total gross privatisation revenue for SSA in 1988-95 (Table 2.2), with the bulk going to Ghana, Nigeria and Zimbabwe (Figure 2.2). For our project countries except South Africa this is even higher (Table 2.2).

Nevertheless, privatisation will not be a magic key to FDI. Most programmes have begun with large utilities (telecoms, water, electricity, transport), or smaller guaranteed profit-makers such as cigarettes (Tanzania selling to RJ Reynolds (US)), breweries (Tanzania to South Africa Breweries) or cement (Zambia's sale of Chilanga). They have liquidated or

Table 2.1 Privatisation Revenues in SSA (1990-96)
(millions of dollars)

	1990	1991	1992	1993	1994	1995	1996	Total
SSA Total	**74**	**1,121**	**207**	**640**	**602**	**472**	**745**	**3,861**
Côte d'Ivoire	..	2	10	5	19	74	103	213
Ghana	10	3	15	28	476	87	186	804
Kenya	12	1	12	10	19	13	137	203
Mozambique	3	5	9	6	2	26	38	89
Nigeria	16	35	114	541	24	..	..	730
South Africa	..	1,073	..	..	..	..	122	1,195
Tanzania	..	..	3	27	5	77	13	125
Uganda	..	..	12	19	24	47	30	132
Zambia	..	..	..	3	14	69	30	115
Zimbabwe	..	..	..	..	13	75	..	88
Other	33	2	32	2	9	5	86	168
Memo: forex generated	***38***	***5***	***66***	***566***	***453***	***275***	***299***	***1,702***

Source:
World Bank, *Global Development Finance 1998*, Vol.1, pp. 108-9, privatisation database and staff estimates.

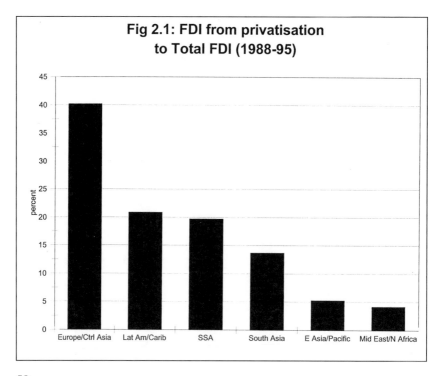

Fig 2.1: FDI from privatisation to Total FDI (1988-95)

Table 2.2 SSA Privatisation Summary (1988-95)
(millions of dollars, unless stated otherwise)

	Revenue	FDI	FDI/Revenue (%)	Number
Benin	54	44	81.5	12
Burkina Faso	0	0	..	1
Burundi	4	0	0.0	8
Cape Verde	0	0	..	1
Côte d'Ivoire	154	26	16.9	24
Ghana	619	451	72.9	52
Guinea Bissau	1	0	0.0	3
Kenya	95	38	40.0	52
Mozambique	52	21	40.4	113
Nigeria	763	500	65.5	58
Sao Tome & Principe	0	0	..	1
South Africa	637	0	0.0	3
Tanzania	111	97	87.4	41
Togo	28	28	100.0	7
Uganda	101	64	63.4	34
Zambia	71	52	73.2	10
Zimbabwe	307	246	80.1	3
Total*	**2,997**	**1,567**	**42.4**	**423**

Notes:
.. figures too small to evaluate.
* numeric average given for FDI/revenue ratio.
Data include all sales of public assets to private entities through public offers, direct sale, contracting out of government services through concessions or licencing agreements, and joint venture arrangements.
Data exclude voucher sales and divestiture and mothballing of SOEs; privatisations under US$50,000; and voucher-based mass privatisations.

Source: World Bank Privatisation Database, in IFC 1997.

sold for virtually nothing a large number of companies, particularly in manufacturing and agriculture. The Zambia study shows graphically how privatisation has been delayed by the absence of functioning stock markets, political opposition to foreign purchasers, technical issues of valuing assets, and complex bidding procedures (which potential foreign investors nevertheless see as non-transparent). After delay has degraded their assets and forced them to be revalued downwards, many companies find few interested buyers, and in final negotiations governments have to take over large amounts of debt, often turning the privatisation into a net foreign exchange loss! Even Zambia Consolidated Copper Mines risks earning less than 30% of its original valuation. While a few prime companies remain to be sold in each country, it is vital to capitalise on these sales with strong positive publicity about wider policies, to mobilise FDI additional to privatisation.

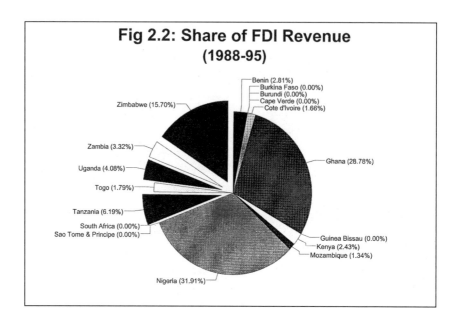

Fig 2.2: Share of FDI Revenue (1988-95)

- Benin (2.81%)
- Burkina Faso (0.00%)
- Burundi (0.00%)
- Cape Verde (0.00%)
- Cote d'Ivoire (1.66%)
- Zimbabwe (15.70%)
- Zambia (3.32%)
- Uganda (4.08%)
- Togo (1.79%)
- Tanzania (6.19%)
- South Africa (0.00%)
- Sao Tome & Principe (0.00%)
- Nigeria (31.91%)
- Ghana (28.78%)
- Guinea Bissau (0.00%)
- Kenya (2.43%)
- Mozambique (1.34%)

2.4.5 Investment Regulations, Promotion and Treaties

Deregulation encourages investors. Restrictive investment codes have been revised in all project countries and across Africa, allowing quicker decision-making, ending commissions or bribes, and creating one-stop investment centres to reduce delay. However, some one-stop centres have become merely an extra level of bureaucracy (UNCTAD, 1995b) with screening for financial viability delayed due to lack of expertise, new inefficient discretionary decisions, or contradictions and disputes between new codes and existing legislation, or their executing agencies. Investors ideally want centres to "hand-hold" them through the bureaucracy of government departments, rather than screening investments. Tanzania's Investment Centre has recently been successfully restructured for a second time with this aim.

Investment promotion centres and their missions to generate funds for particular sectors are widely popular if they are conducted in cooperation with existing investors, who can discuss success stories, focus on examining proposals and detailed preconditions for participation, and help to overcome bureaucratic headaches like work permits or telephone lines. Government also needs to target resources carefully towards probable investors, in preference to blanket large-scale conferences. However, one investor suggested that investment promotion and advice would be better run privately through the local banking system, on the basis that banks might take a longer-term view than government, and would receive funds based only on success.

International treaties and guarantees are rarely cited by investors as important factors. By June 1996 258 bilateral treaties existed between African and capital exporting (mainly developed) countries. All project countries have signed such agreements. They are also all members of multilateral treaties such as the Multilateral Investment Guarantee Authority (MIGA), the International Convention on the Settlement of Investment Disputes (ICSID), and the Convention for the Protection of Industrial Property. Tanzania, Uganda, and Zimbabwe are members of the Convention on Recognition and Enforcement of Foreign Arbitration Awards (UNCTAD, 1997b:xiv; 1996:61, 63; 1995b).

Such agreements indicate commitment to promote and protect FDI, including transfer of payments and profit and capital repatriation, losses from armed conflict or international disorder, nationalisation and expropriation, and dispute settlement. But investors said that they were at most a minor extra safeguard. They cited free trade agreements such as the Lomé Convention as being far more important to their investment decision, especially where they could take advantage of unexploited quotas for exports to the EU. The exception is when source country governments organise investment drives in Africa (for example Malaysia, Brazil, the US) and insist on signature of such agreements as a precondition.

2.5 Political and Social Factors

2.5.1 Political and Social Stability

Political instability is one of the most important criteria affecting investment. Stable government has encouraged investment in Tanzania, Uganda, South Africa, and (until recently) Zimbabwe. Stability need not entail democracy so much as an enabling environment for business. Unfortunately, while investors pay lip service to democracy, they do not care fundamentally who runs the country provided there is strong leadership. One commended Côte d'Ivoire for its death penalty, and another favoured dictatorships for their "rapid decisions", with the view that "democracies in Africa are apparent rather than real". However, anti-democratic moves such as those before the last round of elections in Zambia were acknowledged to generate bad publicity.

But even in stable systems with trusted leaders, foreign investors seem to search desperately for longer-term worries, for example over the "succession" in South Africa and Ghana, or "tribal rivalry" elsewhere. At the back of their minds is the (mis?)perception that stability and effective leadership in black Africa are an aberration. Opinions are also ill-informed and highly subjective. For example one fund manager identified the best prospect in Africa as Kenya, due to strong economic fundamentals and stocks trading at a discount, but another explained this discount was due to political instability.

Investors based in Africa tend to be more realistic and better informed, dismissing most fears as unfounded. They see major advantages to taking a long-term view and maintaining a presence during instability, as this leaves them well placed to resume operations when stability resumes. Those with interests in many countries are best able to spread political risk (Bennell, 1995).

Social instability and crime are equally important. Most potential OECD investors feel they would be unsafe in Africa's cities, in spite of increased policing. Again investors based in Africa are more selective, citing only Johannesburg and Nairobi as more dangerous than London.

2.5.2 Corruption

This is a powerful deterrent to potential OECD investors who, given information constraints and prejudice, see it as endemic across Africa. Those based in Africa tend to be more realistic and better informed, and feel that some types of small-scale and low-level corruption are more efficient than ridiculous taxes or interminable bureaucracy.

Most investors are less forgiving of high-level corruption. "Bleeding the country is Africa's biggest problem", says a British Asian banker with close links to the region. High-profile scandals such as drug smuggling by Zambian ministers or Kenyan politicians buying British firms through Indian firms tarnish the national image and the credibility of economic reform. At middle levels low pay and morale, and high job insecurity for civil servants make corruption more understandable, and many investors suggest urgent salary reviews after removing surplus staff. The most honest investors identify as half the problem a culture within their organisation of paying bribes or petty fraud. Under these circumstances a strong legal framework (as in South Africa) is critical.

Damage through corruption is related to the "credibility" of corruption. As Pfeffermann (1996) argues: "In some fast growing developing economies corruption is commonplace, but is a fairly predictable cost of doing business and bribers can be sure of what they are buying. In contrast, in the majority of developing countries, corruption itself has low credibility — bribers are not sure who to bribe and, most importantly, whether or not they will get what they are seeking to obtain, and this deters all investors, even those who have few scruples about bribery".

This is the crucial issue. The effect on investors depends on their access to information about who to bribe. Smaller investors outside the region face high opportunity costs of obtaining information. Local investors are "more familiar with the way of doing business", and can receive preferential treatment by not paying tariffs or taxes, or tariff protection or monopolies on their goods due to "national or strategic interest". There is a fine line between lobbying and corruption. Trans-national corporations do not hesitate to lobby and offer inducements (political campaign funding, free holidays) where necessary. Some even bribe directly, blaming it on "corrupt bureaucracy and contradictory tax laws". However, they have to watch out for internal auditors or regulations such as the US Foreign Corrupt Practices Act (1978) which fines illicit payments heavily. Though the powers and enforcement of both are often exaggerated, they tend to focus bribery on projects where the transnational corporation can ensure that huge returns will offset any fines.

Western investors have marginally less opportunity to act corruptly. But opinions such as "Western companies are disinvesting from Africa, and are being replaced by smaller Indian outfits with a mind set to endemic corruption" or "British and Europeans are somewhat uptight about corruption which puts them at a competitive disadvantage" bear little resemblance to the truth. A USAID study found only a few dishonest Tanzanian Asians, who give the whole community a bad name (Lofchie and Callaghy, 1995). Instead, these views seem to reflect sour grapes about transnational corporations' slowness in spotting business opportunities and losing out to Asian and South African investors.

2.6 Sector-Specific Factors

Even with favourable economic and political conditions, interest in particular sectors is usually the main driving force determining which countries to invest in. In other words, the success of national efforts to promote FDI depends on natural resources and sector-specific policies.

As shown in Chapter 1, FDI from both traditional and new countries is diversifying into new sectors. Though primary sectors (especially mining and oil) continue to receive most FDI, other sectors such as finance, manufacturing and services are capturing an increasing share (in South Africa, finance, insurance and manufacturing dominate new FDI).

The more dynamic source countries and groups are investing across all sectors. South African investors are putting money into almost every sector. Asian community businesses are also highly diversified across trade, finance and primary and manufactured products. Before the Asian crisis, East Asian companies were investing mainly in non-primary sectors, though post-crisis they have been pulling back because these sectors have suffered. In contrast, OECD investors remain largely wedded to traditional primary sectors.

2.6.1 Primary Sectors

Many SSA countries are endowed with rich natural resource bases, providing huge opportunities in agriculture and mining. Mining is discussed in more detail in Box 2.1. South Asians and Western European investors are heavily involved in agriculture plantations (tea, sugar, cotton). South Africans are strong new competitors, buying farms in neighbouring countries. The biggest growth areas are horticulture and flowers for export. All of our project countries have seen significant expansion in such non-traditional exports during the 1990s. An important negative influence has been commodity price volatility, particularly with the gradual disappearance in the region of marketing board quotas and guaranteed pricing. For example, US FDI in petroleum is vulnerable to oil prices, with companies avoiding new developments or explorations, and paying large dividends to their parents. Location is also important, with investors preferring rich natural resource bases close to manufacturing sites.

Box 2.1 Why Mining and Oil Attract FDI

Mining and petroleum ventures continue to account for the largest proportion of FDI stock and flows in Africa, with dramatic expansion into new countries such as Tanzania and Uganda, Mali, Mauritania and Burkina Faso — as well as new mines in Ghana and Zimbabwe. South African, Australian and Canadian companies feature heavily. Oil also continues to be important for Angola, Cameroon, Congo, Gabon, Nigeria, South Africa and most recently Equatorial Guinea. This sector remains dominated by major OECD oil companies, though Malaysia is investing in South Africa's petroleum sector.

Investment decisions by mining and oil companies are often used as a barometer by businesses in other sectors. One UK mining entrepreneur believes: "we are... the shock troops of investment. If we can invest successfully and harmoniously then we may trigger a move to Africa by international companies which do not need to be in Africa."(World Bank / IMF, *Emerging Markets*, 30/9/96).

However, many factors enable mining companies to overcome problems faced by smaller businesses, through size and diversification. Thus the mining industry views SSA very positively, and is rapidly expanding activity. For example Ashanti has expanded rapidly in the last decade, with mining and prospecting interests in 12 African countries including Ghana, Angola, Ethiopia and Zimbabwe. Anglo-American's restructuring will free resources for mining outside South Africa (which is now one of the most geologically explored parts of the world, and perceived to be in secular decline).

They can invest in their own infrastructure. For example Anglo-American built a water pipeline and employee accommodation at a goldmine in Mali. Needs for extractive industries are so large that self-provision may be more efficient, while other investors expect infrastructure to be provided for them.

They face lower risk. Extractive industries are less exposed to exchange rate risk as they sell almost exclusively on the international market and lodge export proceeds in offshore escrow accounts. They are also experienced in dealing with volatile commodity prices through hedging and forward transactions.

Risk-spreading may be easier. They also reduce their risk by employing small prospecting companies to perform exploration or feasibility studies. These small companies take all initial risk, and are in turn helped by major tax breaks from their home governments.

Financing is more easily available. The primary source is retained earnings, but if a mining company like Anglo-American needs to go to the market, it has a high credit rating and can secure loans against assets abroad, or use its parent company, Minorco's borrowing powers. Mining ventures also find it easier to attract international cofinancing institutions such as CDC and IFC, largely because they have guaranteed streams of hard currency revenues and privileged political status.

Political instability is less worrying for existing investment as mining companies often use their own security forces and infrastructure maintenance. As their projects are strategically vital, they gain access to inside information, and influence political developments. Though they rarely commit new resources under instability, they are rarely obliged to pull out.

2.6.2 Manufacturing

Many relatively new sub-sectors are thriving. **Textiles and footwear** are popular with South Asian and increasingly with South African investors. **Motor and auto-components,** traditionally the preserve of Western European firms, are receiving funds from Korea in South Africa and Botswana, where Hyundai began a vehicle assembly plant in 1996 to service the African market, while South African companies are supplying auto parts and tyres to the region. **Food-processing** is attracting investment from new sources. South Africans are widely involved, and a Chinese firm is planning a cocoa processing plant in Ghana to service the Asian market. **Breweries** are highly lucrative. South Africa Breweries (SAB), the fourth largest in the world, has bought controlling interests in breweries which have been privatised in Tanzania, Zambia, Mozambique, Uganda, Lesotho, Swaziland and Botswana, and set up a virtual regional monopoly, increasing production and introducing new brands. SAB imports effectively reduced Kenya Breweries' production by 20% in 1996, and this is likely to continue with the establishment of a brewery in Thika in late 1998. Huang Gu of China also set up a brewery in Ghana in 1996. **Cigarettes** are another large market, mostly dominated by large TNCs such as RJ Reynolds (which bought Tanzania's privatised company) and BAT. South African and Asian community companies are investing heavily in **soft drink bottling** franchises. **Cement** is proving popular with European and regional investors.

2.6.3 Services

Tourism FDI is growing rapidly, taking advantage of abundant natural resources. Countries with good infrastructure (Zimbabwe) and those without (Zambia) are seeing large new developments. South Africans are involved across the region through chains like Holiday Inn, as are South Asians and Mauritians in Eastern and Southern Africa. The Serena group is a massive investment by the Ismaili Aga Khan. Hong Kong is investing in the Seychelles, and Malaysia in South Africa. This is striking diversification in a sector previously monopolised by Europeans.

In **banking and finance,** South African firms are dominating the region, and providing fierce competition to traditional investors from the West. Standard Bank's purchase of ANZ Grindlay's African section in 1992 under the Stanbic name (in Botswana, Zambia and Zimbabwe, with affiliates in Ghana, Kenya, Nigeria, Uganda and Zaire) means a ready-made presence in many countries, competing effectively with traditional American and British banks. The SA First National Bank also acquired the

Bank of Credit and Commerce in Botswana in 1991. More recently firms have invested in insurance, stockbroking, leasing and merchant banking in Botswana, Namibia and Zimbabwe. South Asians are strong in financial services, most notably banks and foreign exchange bureaux in Kenya, Uganda and Tanzania.

South African **retail** chains are flooding the region, from Zimbabwe through to Kenya, buying up privatised nationwide supermarket networks, though mostly concentrating on the lower end of the market through companies such as Pick 'n' Pay (which for example invested in Zimbabwe's TM Supermarkets in 1995). In East Africa they are even competing successfully with the "regional heavyweight" Uchimi.

South African and Scandinavian companies are leaders in expanding construction activities, with Malaysia and other East Asian and Latin American companies bringing funds into housing and property. Malaysia has also been active in telecommunications in Ghana and South Africa. Private health care and medical supplies are a fast-growing sector for South African and Asian investors, as are radio and television networks and periodicals following the liberalisation of the media in many countries.

2.6.4 Global Sectoral Strategies

One important factor influencing sectoral investment springs from global market trends rather than national endowments: SSA is now competing in a global market on both a country and sector level. Global corporate restructuring has become the trend of the 1990s, particularly among Western and South African TNCs. This involves concentrating on core sectors, shedding diversified projects, in order to maximise comparative advantage and profitability. As examples:

- Unilever's global restructuring in 1994 resulted in selling most of its 40% stake in United Africa Company's Nigerian operations in textiles, timber, air conditioning, and car assembly. In contrast, it increased its holdings in its remaining assets of Lever Brothers Nigeria which were regarded as core business.
- Anglo-American is scaling down non-mining interests in South Africa, built up during the isolation of apartheid, and expanding mining elsewhere in Africa and the world.
- Lonrho has drastically reduced its involvement in non-core sectors, switching from "management by country", which encouraged local knowledge to take advantage of opportunities for diversification, to "management by sector".

2.6.5 Other Factors

Most of the non-sectoral factors which have been discussed earlier in this chapter have varying influences on different sectors, explaining why investors enter some sectors and not others. Four examples will suffice:

- **Economies of scale** in certain sectors enable investors to offset negative national factors. In particular, "strategic" mining and oil activities often continue "even if a country is otherwise falling apart". As discussed in Box 2.1, they continue to be optimistic about Africa. Foreign investors also predominate in certain large-scale sectors (infrastructure, banking etc.) because only they have the start-up capital available from their own funds or international cofinanciers.
- **Treaties** are most useful if they encourage investment in certain sectors, rather than just serve as demonstrations of political goodwill. Agreements between Ghana and Malaysian firms were signed in 1996 covering hotels, banking, real estate, and palm oil development.
- **Risk-sharing** through international cofinancing by banks, international financial institutions or venture capital funds also encourages investment in sectors overlooked by international investors.
- The effects of macro policies on different sectors are also critical. For example, some manufacturing investors argue that **structural adjustment** has hastened disinvestment by manufacturers serving the domestic market, notably through devaluation.

Chapter 3 Portfolio Flows

Nils Bhinda, Stephany Griffith-Jones and Matthew Martin

As shown in Chapter 1, international data assume that portfolio flows come in two main forms: equities and bonds. Within the bond category, this project has identified a key sub-component: foreign purchases of Treasury Bills issued by SSA governments. As equity flows have been by far more important and the fastest growing flow for Sub-Saharan Africa, even exceeding FDI in 1995 (World Bank, 1998), most of the chapter is devoted to their causes, followed by briefer discussions of bonds including Treasury Bills.

3.1 Equity Flows

Portfolio equity flows to SSA have never been systematically analysed: probably because the amounts seem small by global standards and (except for South Africa and Zimbabwe) recent. We conducted comprehensive surveys of specialised African funds, global and emerging market funds, to gauge for the first time the causes of the flows.[1]

3.1.1 Funds and Their Investors

Investment in Africa remains a recent (post-1992) and relatively small field. This reflects low demand from large wholesale investors. Managers of Africa funds have not been reluctant to target large amounts but, with the exception of Morgan Stanley, have not achieved their targets. Nevertheless, their extensive research, sales and marketing work has been bearing fruit during the mid 1990s. Most funds are diversifying across countries and sector, as they gather more knowledge of the region and their perceptions of investment opportunities become more positive.

These efforts to cultivate clients in a "niche market" have protected many against the sharp falls in emerging market portfolio investment in 1997-98.

---

1 It excludes purchases of shares directly in international financial markets (e.g. of SSA companies traded or listed in London or Luxembourg), because data are particularly hard to obtain. These are fairly small, but have increased recently.

Investors are split roughly evenly between retail and institutions, and the US and UK are the main sources. Evidence from other emerging markets suggests this may bring greater volatility, as Anglo-Saxon (especially US) investors focus more on short-term returns than those from continental Europe. However, some funds (e.g. the Africa Emerging Markets Fund) do attract European and Middle Eastern investors. Framlington and Regent are trying to reduce volatility by targeting local investors and institutions for joint ventures (and for Regent by listings in Kenya and Botswana).

Donor involvement has also been a powerful incentive for diversification and local investment. For example, Framlington targeted the Caisse Française de Développement (CFD) and the IFC. Donors often have the resources to overcome the "information deficit" on Africa, allowing the private sector to receive accurate information without investing resources. But donor involvement raises the question of whether the funds are entirely "private" capital flows.

Another reason for lower volatility of flows to SSA is that 85% have come via closed-end funds (Table 1.4). By their nature, such funds should reduce volatility because they are relatively protected from actual and exempted redemptions by individual investors, as claims are traded on a developed country stock exchange, and are not, like open-ended funds, required to redeem claims on demand. However, the Mexican peso crisis indicates only a marginal effect of closed-end funds on volatility (Griffith-Jones, 1996; IMF, 1995).

3.1.2 Global Factors

Global or "push" factors were extremely important to the rapid rise in portfolio equity in the mid-1990s as part of a broader OECD trend to invest in emerging markets. Among our project countries, these factors have impacted most strongly on South Africa, which is most closely tied to the international economy, and then filtered through to the region.

Globally, the growing asset base of institutional investors, due to huge rises in pension funds, (reflecting a higher ratio of aged to active population in the industrial countries), is dramatically increasing aggregate savings in portfolio flows. In the longer term, this may well be offset by a slowdown in growth of the labour force, and therefore a decline in returns on capital relative to labour. Relaxed regulation is encouraging pension funds to become the "major force in further international diversification and, in particular, in the demand for portfolio equities from developing countries" (World Bank, 1997a:113-123). Declines in international interest rates have triggered huge movements (Calvo *et al*, 1991, 1993, and 1995; Asea and Reinhart, 1995; Chuhan *et al*, 1993; Fernandez-Arias, 1994).

Cyclical downturn in developed countries has also reduced economic activity, and demand for investment funds.

In this context, the most important factor encouraging flows to Africa was risk diversification in search of higher returns, encouraged by low correlation between rates of return in industrial countries (particularly the US and UK) and those in emerging markets. The Morgan Stanley and IFC indices indicated throughout this period tremendous scope for increasing returns through diversification (World Bank, 1997a). SSA markets provided more scope for high returns from diversification, due to low correlation with other emerging markets, in turn reflecting the low levels of flows to SSA. Furthermore, price/earnings ratios in SSA were very low, making shares "undervalued" and overcoming expectations of higher risk and lower growth.

In addition, stock exchanges were much less correlated within SSA than within Latin America (*Emerging Market Investor*, June 1996). For example, Zimbabwe's exchange responds largely to national events, making Zimbabwe more likely to benefit from investors seeking to diversify out of South Africa. At the other extreme, Namibia's exchange is seen as "little more than an adjunct to the Johannesburg exchange, as most stocks have dual listings" (*World Equity*, 2/97:51).

This low correlation has also largely insulated SSA from global financial crises (Mexico 1995; Asia, Russia and Brazil 1997-9), making its stock exchanges less volatile. For example, the Botswana and Zimbabwe exchanges are weakly correlated with the US and Latin America, even though Latin American countries are implementing similar macro and trade reform (Jefferis *et al*, 1997). However, South Africa's short-term links with emerging and developed markets are stronger, due to its weight in fund managers' portfolios, the size of the equity market and its more efficient transmission of signals and shocks (Jefferis *et al*, 1997).

In the mid-1990s, flows to South Africa rose sharply, as did its correlations with world markets and therefore its volatility. Flows, correlations and volatility also rose for other SSA countries as capital markets were liberalised. Many Africa funds invested a disproportionately small amount in South Africa relative to market capitalisation (90% of the region) or GDP (45%) weights (Table 1.5), in order to diversify within the region in search of higher returns from "undervalued and high growth assets" and "frontier" markets (see *Africa Emerging Markets 1998;* Regent, 1998). Increased volatility reflected onward "contagion" from South Africa and increased flows. Countries are therefore faced with policy dilemmas: there is a trade-off between higher flows and increased regional integration, and higher volatility.

As recent crises have shown once again, flows often do not reflect economic fundamentals, so that problems in one country (or group) cause contagion in perfectly healthy economies by leading investors to reappraise exposure to all emerging markets. These unstable cycles of euphoria and pessimism will hit SSA harder as it integrates financially into the world economy.

However, the "herd behaviour" among investors which causes volatility can occasionally be a stabilising influence. For example one fund manager did not pull out of South Africa after the collapse of the rand and the South African stock exchange in mid-1996, because the share of South African stocks in the IFC and Morgan Stanley indices was fairly large. As many of his colleagues invested in line with these indices, he would have performed below average if the South African stock market recovered. An important precondition for attracting and sustaining portfolio flows is the inclusion of SSA markets in key indices, chiefly IFC's.

3.1.3 Perceptions of Sub-Saharan Africa

Perceptions of SSA affect the extent to which increased flows to emerging markets are channelled to the region. These range widely from negative bias, to those who see SSA as "the final frontier" and "the last region of opportunity". Negative perceptions of Africa are a major cause of under-investment. They are based on a mixture of real concerns (discussed below) and a large element of misinterpretation of signals (and in particular, dismissal of new positive trends), and use of irrelevant benchmarks.

Perceptions vary by type of investor. Pan-African fund managers tend to be more "Afro-realistic", and were generally very positive with better informed views of the region. Global fund managers become "Afro-euphoric" when things go well, and "Afro-pessimistic" at other times: they acknowledge their lack of information by urging Africa to "sell itself more", and saying that it receives "a raw deal in the media". Swings in mood are therefore closely tied to quality and quantity of information. The more investors diversify, the less information they have to support their decisions (Calvo and Mendoza, 1995), especially in smaller markets where information collection is more expensive and exposure is small. As one fund manager put it, "there is nobody in the main investment banks or fund managers who has any real experience in Africa: often there is no dedi-cated investment manager for the African continent". This traps many SSA countries in a vicious circle of poor information, low expectation, and low investment.

But even fund managers with better information and optimism about SSA are unwilling to invest due to the way their performance is judged. All managers are assessed on short-term benchmarks (on average three months), even though they are investing long-term assets such as pension funds. Thus individual willingness to take a long-term position may be overridden by pressures not to stray from the herd. This is worsened by perceived volatility of economic policy and performance in SSA, which could (over the short-term horizon) lead a fund with high SSA exposure to underperform, losing money from their clients. It will remain hard for SSA countries to attract huge portfolio flows until a large group of investors changes perceptions fundamentally.

3.1.4 National Factors

Many national influences are shared with foreign direct investors, and have been treated in more detail in Chapter 2. The positive influences most often cited were political stability; low levels of corruption and bureaucracy; commitment to private ownership and attracting foreign flows; strong growth; well coordinated economic policy; regional economic integration to overcome problems of small market size; regional structures for commercial banks as in the CFA Zone with common supervision and regulation (Mistry, 1996); a young and motivated labour force; rich primary resources; and efficient transport and telecom networks. On the basis of these factors, Mauritius, Ivory Coast, Botswana and Zimbabwe were often cited more positively than Latin American or Asian markets during interviews with fund managers in 1996-97.

Portfolio investors also have specific concerns, the most important of which are the development of stock exchanges, perceptions of individual countries, a collection of portfolio-specific macroeconomic indicators, and the presence of donor support for portfolio investment:

Since 1989, many SSA countries have established or expanded stock exchanges, as part of a policy of integration into the international financial market, and of attracting foreign private capital to overcome inefficient local financial intermediation and stimulate savings and investment (Jaspersen et al, 1996). Of the 15 SSA exchanges, 10 have been established in the last decade. Another five countries are considering starting their own exchanges. In order to expand the market and increase economies of scale, the stock exchange in Abidjan has been expanded to cover seven countries in the Francophone West African sub-region.

Exchanges are perceived as vastly preferable to trading of large African companies' shares in international markets such as London or Luxembourg. While this widens the investor appeal of African shares, it tends to slow development of local exchanges. For example Ashanti's listing of its stock on the London market caused a substantial rapid transfer of turnover from Ghana to London, to benefit from price differentials.

Exchanges serve an important function because fund managers prefer to (or are legally required to) invest in listed companies. Some invest in unlisted companies if there is the possibility to on-sell, or they are about to be listed, because they offer higher returns. Perceptions vary: the Mauritius Fund invests 20% unlisted, but the Africa Emerging Markets Fund only 5% of a permitted 30%.

Positive performance by stock exchanges has been a powerful attraction for portfolio flows, periodically provoking "Afro-euphoria" among investors (for example for Nigeria, Ivory Coast, Zimbabwe and Namibia in 1995/6). This performance has reflected the expansion of privatisation programmes; the suspension / abolition of capital gains tax in most SSA countries, and reduction of withholding tax on dividends; strong dealing systems; the absence of exchange controls; and especially the presence of strong natural resources, all of which offset the lack of market size. As a result of these factors, investors see opportunities in copper and sugar in Zambia; in minerals in Botswana; and in many sectors in Uganda.

However, several factors hold back the growth of stock exchanges outside South Africa (for more details, see Emenuga, 1997; N'Guessan, 1997):

• lack of indigenous listed companies. This reflects aversion by indigenous entrepreneurs to go public for fear of losing control, and their lack of experience and resources to float their companies (Emenuga, 1997:158; Alile and Anao, 1986). Low domestic levels of savings and investment (due to weak financial infrastructure, and inefficient resource allocations and wealth distribution) also hinder domestic involvement. Low local participation is seen as reflecting lack of confidence, discouraging foreigners. High local participation boosts credibility and moderates the volatility of fickle international flows. The Abidjan exchange has overcome this to some degree by encouraging a "second market" with less strict listing requirements and an over-the-counter unlisted market.

• small average company size. However, this is misleading in some countries, where a few large companies account for most capitalisation, such as Ghana's Ashanti Goldfields.

• low capitalisation — but this doubled in 1993-5, bringing capitalisation/GNP ratios to the same level as many other emerging and developed country exchanges (IFC, 1998:18).

• low liquidity as measured through the turnover ratio (the value of shares traded as a proportion of capitalisation). This has been found by analysts to be the factor linking stock exchanges with economic growth (Levine and Zervos, 1996; Jefferis et al, 1997) — though it can also reduce volatility of flows. Low liquidity puts off foreign investors, because it may prevent them from selling their shares, and may cause volatility if trades are dominated by a small number of large privatisations. Even the

Johannesburg Stock Exchange, despite being the largest emerging market in terms of capitalisation, has long been one of the least liquid. Several exchanges have been introducing Treasury Bills, government bonds, CDs and corporate bonds onto markets to increase liquidity.

Low liquidity is due to the dominance of holdings by the original direct investors, the public sector, and local institutional investors, who have a "buy-and-hold" attitude; historical or continuing exchange controls; delays in settlement processes; excessive regulation; high official or "corrupt" transaction costs including taxes; sharp practice or corruption/fraud by brokers; short trading hours (averaging 2 for about 2-5 days per week); official limits on price fluctuations (to discourage speculation); a small number of listings; and the low frequency or absence of external auditing of accounts. Many countries have tackled these problems in 1995-9. In conjunction with privatisations and openness to non-resident investors, this has dramatically increased liquidity (see Emenuga, 1997; and N'Guessan, 1997).

Several macroeconomic issues are crucial to portfolio investors. The fundamental balance (the current account deficit minus FDI, which indicates balance of payments sustainability) is generally negative for SSA. Monetary policy is a crucial indicator of liquidity, suggesting likely future trends in share prices: investors would prefer looser policy to increase liquidity, provided this did not lead to exchange rate falls, higher inflation, collapses in reserves or the ending of an IMF programme. The soundness of the banking system which in most African countries (as discussed in Chapter 4 in more detail) is inefficient, undercapitalised and burdened with overhangs of domestic bad debt is a key deterrent to portfolio investment (see also Mistry, 1996). Exchange rate prospects influence investors both by affecting projected dollar values of investments and by influencing targets (for example encouraging export-oriented industries if devaluation seems likely).

Finally, given the underdevelopment of most African stock exchanges, macroeconomic problems, and volatile investor perceptions, donor support for portfolio funds or technical assistance (for example to help companies list on stock exchanges) has been valuable to increasing portfolio flows. Such assistance is provided through organisations like IFC, CDC, Proparco and the EIB. Though they are small (maximum $25 million), due to their regional knowledge, donor funds are better at identifying opportunities, giving comfort to private investors (both domestic and foreign) and other official investors (for example the CDC's 10-year Commonwealth Africa Investment Fund, COMAFIN, created in 1996, has major participation from institutional investors in Malaysia, Singapore, the Brunei Investment Agency, the Development Bank of Southern Africa,

Botswana, Mauritius and Zimbabwe). They also tend to widen the sectors considered by investors (beyond natural resources to services, tourism and private infrastructure); the number of countries receiving investment (even extending to countries such as Mozambique which as yet have no stock exchanges); and the number of companies insofar as they focus mainly on unlisted companies. They often participate actively on company boards, acting more like venture capitalists. As funds are small, success is measured by whether investments will complement rather than crowd out private sector foreign or local investment.

On the downside, investors say donors lack business understanding, and are "reliant on number crunching" with "poor understanding of the rationale for a project". They possess a "lender's mentality, trying to plug the downside at any cost", which "clouds understanding of risk and reward". They are also inefficient due to bureaucracy, options, and shareholder agreements, which are easy to avoid when things go bad, and "encourage poor promoters". Recipient countries complain that they tend to focus mainly on expanding privatised companies, and that the scale of investments ($0.5-10 million) is too large for most indigenous companies.

3.1.5 Sectoral Factors

Investors target strong and undervalued sectors within countries, in order to diversify risk and increase return. Some funds (such as Morgan Stanley) are highly diversified across sectors, but others show clear bias towards particular sectors. Consumer goods and services, considered "less volatile", constitute a third of total portfolio for Mercury and Alliance Capital, and many funds see high potential here. Low-cost, volume-driven primary sectors such as mining and agriculture, and agro-business are targeted as traditionally profitable areas. Regent allocates a third of its portfolio here, Mercury 17% and Alliance 13%. Newly privatised companies such as telecoms, power and infrastructure, breweries and cement are seen as "sure bets". Tourism has immense prospects across the region and particularly for Mauritius, where the Mauritius Fund invests 19%. Banking is very popular in some countries including Mauritius, which is set to become an offshore tax haven for South Africa and other states with high tax regimes. The Mauritius Fund has 27% invested; Morgan Stanley 10%, and Alliance 13% in financial services.

3.2 Non-Equity Flows

Non-equity portfolio instruments (bonds and Treasury Bills) have rapidly become key sources of flows to SSA in the mid-1990s, due to the liberalisation of external and domestic financial transactions. Almost all portfolio funds have considerable exposure in both types of instruments, though exact figures are unavailable due to information constraints. Many funds initiate their investments by focussing on non-equity instruments. In 1995-97 they increased their equity holdings in response to stock market development and global market trends; but in 1998-9, as part of a more global "flight from equity", many reduced the equity holdings and switched to bonds and T-Bills.

3.2.1 Bonds

Fixed income debt instruments (particularly bonds) are often dollar denominated, which implies no currency risk for the dollar-based investor. They comprise new internationally issued bonds, and debt reduction instruments.

New bonds have included a wealth of public and private sector issues from South Africa; Mauritius' first issue in 1995 to finance infrastructure; and Ghana's convertible private sector bond from Ashanti Goldfields. Most have been highly successful (Ashanti's bond was increased from $175m to $250m due to demand, largely from US institutional investors).

The key factors determining the success of bond issues (measured in terms of full or over-subscription and therefore reasonably low spreads over benchmark US bond yields) are positive foreign investor perceptions of country credit risk (influenced partly in turn by credit ratings as discussed in Chapter 5 below); and their changing willingness to take risks in emerging markets — rather than retreating to even more secure developed market bonds.

Fixed income bonds related to debt reduction include Brady bonds in Nigeria and IDA debt reduction bonds in other countries, and promissory notes for other debt. But these are mostly traded on secondary markets, typically in London or New York, and do not generate a net capital inflow into SSA (though if the debt prices in secondary markets rise, this can improve a country's creditworthiness, making it easier to attract other capital flows).

Foreign investment in domestic bonds has been a dominant — and highly volatile — form of capital flow into South Africa in recent years. Table 3.1 shows that bond trading volumes by non-residents have soared since 1995, with gross purchases and sales increasing 40-fold to reach their

Table 3.1 Transactions by Non-Residents on the Bond Exchange of South Africa
(millions of South African Rand)

	1994	1995	1996	1997	1998
Gross Purchases	22,897	35,299	175,138	605,992	1,371,526
Gross Sales	22,479	33,130	171,755	591,214	1,381,291
Net Purchases	1,103	1,871	3,383	14,778	-9,765

Source: South African Reserve Bank.

massive 1998 levels. Net purchases also rose dramatically, more than quad-rupling between 1996 and 1997, only to plummet to large net sales in 1998. The causes underlying these trends are discussed below.

Huge increases in non-resident trading resulted from push factors including the normalisation of international financial relations and port-folio diversification by international investors, and critical pull factors including the abolition of the Financial Rand (March 1995) which ended the dual exchange rate system, high domestic interest rates and a series of far reaching reforms to the trading system (Ncube, Leape and Thomas, 1996). Reforms to the bond market began in 1995 with the introduction of a net settlement system, simplification of settlement arrangements, immo-bilisation of the scrip of major traded stocks at the central depository, adoption of an electronic trading system, and tightening of listing require-ments to emphasise full disclosure. In 1996, the Bond Market Association was converted into a formal exchange (the Bond Exchange of South Africa). Subsequent reforms included the shift from a "second Thursday" settlement period to the international standard of three day rolling settle-ment (T+3). A further pull factor stimulating portfolio investment in recent years is the use of South African bonds as an instrument to hedge liabilities in the growing Eurorand market, in which Rand denominated debt is issued and traded internationally.

The contagion effects of the Asian crisis were, at times, severe. While South Africa continued to experience record inflows during the first phase of the crisis, Figure 3.1 shows there were massive net bond sales by non-residents in October 1997, when the effects of the collapse of the Hong Kong market were felt (Khatri and Leape, 1997). In the wake of the Asian crisis, as the major markets began to recover lost ground, foreign invest-ment in South African bonds resumed, only to experience sharp volatility in mid-1998 with the crises in Russia and Indonesia (see Box 3.1).

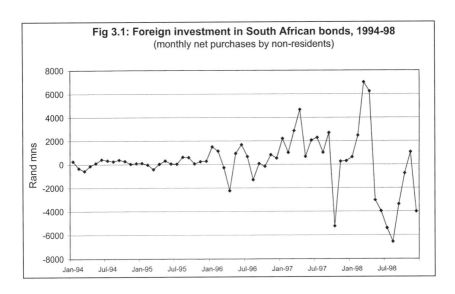

Fig 3.1: Foreign investment in South African bonds, 1994-98
(monthly net purchases by non-residents)

Box 3.1 The Effects of the Asia Crisis on Southern Africa

The "contagion" of the Asia crisis to South Africa and to a lesser extent Zimbabwe shows how the perceptions of international investors can become detached from national reality and be driven instead by developments in other emerging markets. The financial sector crisis in the ASEAN countries was characterised by rapidly depreciating currencies and collapsing asset prices. Its spread to South Africa and also Zimbabwe occurred when the crisis extended beyond the region, to take on global ramifications. The contagion can be analysed in two phases. The first immediately followed the Thai liquidity crisis in mid-1997 and lasted to October 1997. The effects were limited to a handful of neighbouring countries, who were subjected to a reassessment of risks on the grounds both of similarities in relevant characteristics with Thailand, and of vulnerability to direct effects. Figures 3.2a-c show that this phase had no significant effect on either South Africa or Zimbabwe, with their IFC investables indices maintaining their value at a time when the Asian index began its sharp decline. South Africa continued to experience record inflows of foreign investment in bonds and equity. Its resilience at this stage is evidence that international investors judged that in key areas — including exchange rate policy, the soundness of the banking sector and the sustainability of the external position — South Africa did

79

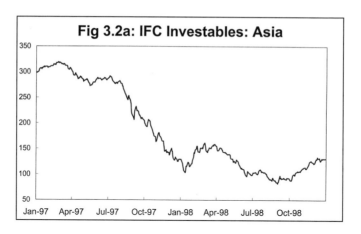

Fig 3.2a: IFC Investables: Asia

Fig 3.2b: IFC Investables: South Africa

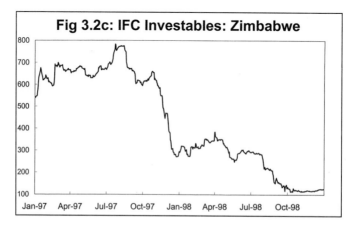

Fig 3.2c: IFC Investables: Zimbabwe

not share the weaknesses identified in the core ASEAN countries. South Africa and Zimbabwe did, however, feel the effects of the second phase, along with virtually all developed and emerging markets previously insulated from the crisis. Precipitous declines in the stock markets and exchange rates of Thailand, Malaysia, the Philippines and Indonesia led to increasing pressure on the Hong Kong market and the dollar peg. Sustained speculative pressure forced the authorities to raise interest rates sharply, squeezing investors and rendering downward pressure on the Hang Seng irresistible. By October, this triggered crashes in the major equity markets, which fed through to South Africa and Zimbabwe (Figures 3.2b-c). As Asia showed modest signs of recovery before dropping further in April 1998, South Africa made a significant recovery to pre-crisis levels, and Zimbabwe more moderately, before slumping again. That South Africa was affected by the second phase of contagion is explained, in part, by the historically high correlation between returns on the Johannesburg Stock Exchange (JSE) and the stock markets in the US and the UK (contrasting with the low correlations with ASEAN markets). But the effects of the second phase were also driven by two global processes: first, a re-rating by international investors of broad asset classes (including emerging market debt and equity), and second, an increase in investors' risk aversion, reflected on a more global level in a reduced demand for risky assets such as equity.

As shown in Figure 3.1, the large inflows into the South African bond market in the first three quarters of 1997 were sharply reversed in October, with non-resident sales that month of R5.3bn — equivalent to one percent of GDP. In contrast, although prices on the JSE fell dramatically, foreign investors continued to be net purchasers of South African equities. Monthly net non-resident purchases peaked at R3.8bn, as cheaper shares were seen as "bargains". Although the rand depreciated by 6% against the US dollar between July and October, the sharp appreciation of the rand in the first quarter of 1997 meant that the depreciation over the year to the end of October was only 2.8 percent — in contrast to the sharp depreciations in the core ASEAN economies. Offsetting portfolio equity inflows help to explain the limited impact of the October crash on the rand's external value. Figure 3.1 also shows how South Africa was affected by what might be termed a third phase of the crisis in mid-1998. The collapses in Russia and Indonesia in May 1998 triggered a sharp reversal in foreign bond investment, as cumulative inflows in excess of 2% of GDP in March and April were followed by cumulative outflows of 3% of GDP in the next four months.

As South Africa and Zimbabwe compete in different markets to the Asian economies, the effect on trade competitiveness is limited in the short term. In the longer term, Asian exporters might compete directly with South Africa and Zimbabwe in the Africa region, although this will be affected by additional factors including labour costs, and the pace of product and market development in non-traditional exports. The effects on the composition of South Africa's and Zimbabwe's trade partners are also likely to be minimal, as the affected ASEAN economies are not important export markets (e.g., they accounted for only 2% of South Africa's non-gold exports in 1996) while South Africa's and Zimbabwe's main trading partners in Europe and Africa were largely unaffected by the crisis. More generally, falls in gold and coal prices adversely affected South Africa as a major producer, but lower oil prices reduced import costs in both South Africa and Zimbabwe, mitigating potential losses in export receipts on the current account. As Malaysia was a major source of new FDI flows to both countries and South Korea a potential source, the crisis has also had adverse effects on inward investment from these sources.

What can South Africa and Zimbabwe learn from the crisis? Perhaps most obviously, the events of recent months serve as a reminder that crises are costly. Even with bailouts, the adjustments required by financial crises have massive real costs. Moreover, in contrast to Mexico and the ASEAN countries, Africa has no "big brother" to facilitate a bailout in the first place. Looking forward, the Asian crisis highlights the need for attention in four policy areas. The first is *exchange rate policy*. The Asian currency pegs left the current accounts vulnerable to external developments such as the relative strength of the US dollar. Further, the pegs acted as implicit guarantees on the value of domestic assets, encouraging external borrowing, which leads to the second policy area of *debt management*. The Asian crisis highlights the dangers of large unhedged foreign currency debt and an inappropriate maturity structure. The third area is *financial regulation and supervision*. The Asian crisis has again underscored the need to put in place a sound regulatory framework when the implicit regulation contained in exchange controls is removed with liberalisation. The final area relates to the role of *transparency*: the timely and accurate availability of key indicators. Transparency works to pre-empt crises by enhancing the proper functioning of markets, encouraging inward investment and promoting policy discipline.

Source: Khatri and Leape, 1997.

3.2.2 Treasury Bills

Domestically-issued Treasury Bills are another increasingly attractive opportunity for foreigners in SSA. Banks invested heavily in T-Bills for foreign clients in the early 1990s in Tanzania, Uganda and Zambia. This provided "easy money for the banks when no lending was being done", and a "sure bet" for their customers. Newly launched portfolio funds also purchased T-Bills as a "short-term home" for cash while they identified equity projects — but very often these "Africa" funds invested in non-SSA T-Bills (Table 1.5).

The most important factor causing forex inflows to purchase T-Bills has been interest rate differentials with international investments, notably high domestic interest rates in Tanzania (Kimei *et al*, 1997:11), Uganda and Zambia. These high interest rates have been particularly attractive when exchange rates are projected to appreciate or stay constant, but have sometimes even overcome fears of exchange rate depreciation. The interest rates have been doubly attractive because the inverted yield curves of underdeveloped government debt markets, especially when governments are borrowing heavily for 91 days to fund budget deficits, have made rates highest on the short-term instruments which provide less term risk.

In addition, some of the "foreign" purchases have been by returning emigrants (especially Asians) based in the region who can interpret market signals more rapidly and minimise risk. They have inspired large capital flows playing on arbitrage gains from relative trends in exchange rates and T-Bill interest rates in Kenya, Tanzania and Uganda since all three markets were liberalised. As such flows are virtually impossible to track (often entering through foreign exchange bureaux), their scale cannot be reliably estimated, but transactions have often reached several million dollars per week. Many purchases are funded from foreign currency accounts (FCAs) maintained by nationals, implying that these flows may not be genuinely "foreign" and may simply represent "re-use" of forex purchased from other sources.

However, investors have been wary in conditions of "excessive borrowing" leading to perceived default or rollover risk, notably in pre-election periods when governments tend to borrow excessively. Interest rates have also tended to vary sharply with inflation, and real interest rates have fallen over time if inflation stays low for long periods (as in Uganda). Purchases have fallen sharply in most SSA countries as post-liberalisation booms in interest rates subside.

T-Bill purchases have therefore been marked by a high degree of volatility. Fortunately, given the instability in T-Bill markets, most investors in SSA have believed that "T-Bills are no way to build up a business base" and therefore foreign holdings of T-Bills have not risen to levels where their withdrawal has undermined government finance, the exchange rate, the balance of payments and the banking system (as in the Mexican peso crisis — see Griffith-Jones, 1996). However, in some SSA countries (Tanzania, Uganda, Zambia), bank exposure in T-Bills with falling interest rates has exacerbated weak balance sheets and contributed to banking collapses. It is worrying that African governments are often neither monitoring nor analysing these flows.

Chapter 4 Bank Flows

Nils Bhinda, Stephany Griffith-Jones and Matthew Martin

As discussed in Chapter 1, international data show no discernible increase in medium-term bank lending to Sub-Saharan Africa in the 1990s; though short-term debt has had a more positive recent trend. Country data indicate that bank flows have been increasing for almost all project countries — and short-term flows unguaranteed by OECD export credit agencies have risen sharply. If continued, this trend will mean a worrying shortening of the maturity profile, potentially increasing country vulnerability to financial crisis. What explains stagnation of long-term flows except in South Africa, and the rise in short-term flows?

4.1 Structure of the Banking System

One major influence on lending is the continued dominance of foreign banks in our project countries, and their attitudes and client base. The pattern of banking in many countries changed dramatically in the 1980s and early 1990s, with the results shown in Table 4.1.

In some countries — notably Francophone Africa — foreign banks have sharply reduced or rationalised their presence, with British banks closing most of their branches. The French also sold their flagship bank, the BIAO. Nevertheless, banking in many Francophone countries remains dominated by French banks (see Njinkeu, 1997). As of 1997, three French banking groups held 50% of the total bank capital in the BECAO region. At a country level, they also dominate the markets in Burkina Faso (74%); Togo (67%); Senegal (65%) and Côte d'Ivoire (63%); and to a lesser extent in Niger (41%) and Mali (40%). Crédit Lyonnais and Banque Nationale de Paris are also significant shareholders in the banks of Cameroon, Chad and Gabon, though reform of the banking sector has reduced their holdings, and they have no presence in Congo or the Central African Republic.

On the other hand in countries which have privatised and liberalised banking sectors (such as Ghana, Kenya, Mozambique, Tanzania, Uganda and Zambia), many new foreign banks have been established, and existing banks have expanded their branch networks. Citibank has branches in 10 countries; Equator Bank, a subsidiary of HSBC which specialises in SSA, in 8; and Standard Chartered in 11. Once again, South African banks are

Table 4.1 International Banking Presence in SSA

	BNP	Barclays	Citibank	Credit Lyonnais	Equator	Société Générale	Stanbic	Standard Chartered
Total Countries	6	11	10	8	8	3	15	11
Total Branches	**	258*	10	**	8	**	**	138
Angola	-	-	-	-	1(r)	-	-	-
Benin	-	-	-	**	-	-	-	-
Botswana	-	34(s)	-	-	-	-	**(s)	15(s)
Burkina Faso	**	-	-	-	-	-	-	-
Cameroon	**	-	1	**	-	**	-	3(s)
Chad	-	-	-	**	-	-	-	-
Congo DR	-	-	1	-	-	-	**(s)	-
Côte d'Ivoire	**	-	1	**	1(r)	**	-	-
Gabon	**	-	1	**	-	-	-	-
The Gambia	-	-	-	-	-	-	-	5(s)
Ghana	-	27(s)	-	-	1(r)	-	**(a)	20(s)
Kenya	-	92(s)	1	-	1(r)	-	**(s)	31(s)
Lesotho	-	-	-	-	-	-	**(s)	-
Madagascar	-	-	-	-	-	-	**(a)	-
Mali	-	-	-	**	-	-	-	-
Mauritius	-	20(b)	-	-	-	-	-	-
Mozambique	-	-	-	-	1(r)	-	**(a)	-
Namibia	-	-	-	-	-	-	**(s)	-
Nigeria	-	1(r)	1	-	-	-	**(s)	-
Senegal	**	-	1	**	-	**	-	-
Seychelles	-	7(b)	-	-	-	-	-	-
Sierra Leone	-	2(s)	-	-	-	-	-	(1(s))
South Africa	-	**	1	-	1(r)	-	771	1(r)
Swaziland	-	-	-	-	-	-	**(s)	-
Tanzania	-	-	1	-	-	-	**(s)	3(s)
Togo	**	-	-	**	-	-	-	-
Uganda	-	2(s)	-	-	1(r)	-	**(s)	1(s)
Zambia	-	15(s)	1	-	1(r)	-	**(s)	14(s)
Zimbabwe	-	49(s)	-	-	-	-	**(s)	44(s)

Notes:
Legal status of country head office (where known):
s - subsidiary of PLC, with HQ shareholding
b - branch of HQ
r - representative office
a - associate bank
* - excludes South Africa
** - number of branches not known.
Number in brackets denotes branch not operational.

Sources:
Information on Anglophone banks supplied by London offices and bank reports.
Information on Francophone banks in Njinkeu, 1997.

also expanding rapidly into the region, notably Standard Bank of South Africa (Stanbic), which purchased the African division of ANZ Grindlays, placing itself in a strong position to compete for corporate and retail banking business with the historically dominant Barclays and Standard Chartered. First National Bank also bought BCCI in Botswana in 1991.

International banks dominate foreign currency deposits and lending in virtually all Sub-Saharan countries. There are three main explanations:

- they tend to manage virtually all of the donor, embassy and NGO funds (whether project-related or administrative accounts), which provide large foreign currency profits;
- they have much better links with international correspondent banks and are therefore able to access credit lines and conduct foreign exchange transactions more easily;
- because of the first two factors, and their international "cachet", they tend to attract foreign currency transactions and deposits from local companies and rich individuals.

However, they are highly cautious lenders, tending to favour blue-chip companies such as the largest multinationals and local corporates, and high net worth foreign and local individuals. Multinationals are most popular because of a "global relationship banking" system where subsidiaries can secure lending, on the basis of a letter of comfort from their HQ and their dealings with the bank elsewhere. While this has worked as a long-run strategy for maximising returns and reducing risk, one or two banks have "taken a beating on this", and now prefer to examine the creditworthiness of local subsidiaries separately. Most multinational banks view national and smaller companies with suspicion, even for short-term finance.

4.2 Term of Lending

The wish of lenders to change exposure in response to economic trends is the most powerful influence on lending trends, as reflected by the term of lending.

It has led to a rapid recent rise in short-term lending, particularly trade financing, which all bankers interviewed in Africa and London consider their "core lending growth area" in SSA. The main cause of this rise has been improving export performance (for example in Zimbabwe, Tanzania and Uganda), because most lending is pre-export finance, secured by the exports themselves via the assigning of export contracts or escrow accounts for the export receipts. It is most common for minerals (copper and cobalt in Zambia, platinum and gold in Zimbabwe), petroleum, and agricultural commodities (coffee in Tanzania and Uganda). A few of the most reputable export companies, with their own stocks of foreign exchange in deposit accounts, are also able to obtain import finance (e.g. Anglo, Lonrho and ZCCM in Zambia). Nevertheless, in order to maintain their ability to change exposure, and because of worries about longer-term risk, banks often use rollovers of such short-term facilities to keep good customers happy while refusing them medium-term loans.

All such credit is short-term, seasonal where appropriate, and lasts 90-180 days. As elsewhere in the developing world, it is highly volatile: even though the loans are largely "self-liquidating", banks monitor commodity production or price changes closely and rollovers are frequently denied. Two collapses in capital flows to South Africa in 15 years were provoked by reduction in trade lines (Leape, 1991; Aron and Elbadawi, forthcoming). Credit is also procyclical, rushing in when commodity prices boom (as with coffee in Uganda) and out when they fall. It therefore exacerbates macroeconomic instability.

On the other other hand, medium-term loans have fallen throughout the last ten years, as maturing loans have not been replaced by new flows. Only a few countries (Botswana, Congo, Ghana, Kenya, Mauritius, Namibia, Tanzania, Uganda, Zambia, Zimbabwe) have attracted funds, and nearly all of these have been related to specific export-oriented mining or oil projects or major privatisations involving foreign investors, where term lending is seen as less risky.

4.3 Local Sources of Foreign Exchange

A third important factor reducing foreign exchange inflows for bank lending has been the rapidly increasing amount of foreign exchange held within the African economy's banking system, removing the need to call on foreign credit lines or correspondent banks. Traditionally, banks had relied on donor, embassy or NGO funds, which were virtually inaccessible for forex lending and highly volatile in response to political or economic instability.

In the 1990s, liberalisation of foreign exchange regulations by SSA governments has led to rapid growth in foreign currency accounts (FCAs) held by resident companies and individuals, which partly represents the return of flight capital. As explained by many banks in interviews, this gives banks a large pool of domestically held foreign exchange to draw upon for lending. Though firm data are not available, bankers estimate that it accounts for tens of millions of dollars in each of the many SSA countries with large foreign currency account holdings. It may explain why the rise in short-term foreign exchange lending is not reflected in the cross-border lending figures published by international institutions. Unfortunately, by replacing lending from bank headquarters, lending from FCAs is hiding creditworthy demand in Africa from the international community. But in the longer term it might translate into further return of flight capital and improved perceptions of creditworthiness.

4.4 Domestic Financial Sector Conditions

Domestic financial sector conditions are among the most fundamental influences on foreign currency lending. The previous chapter provided one reason why banks have little need to undertake foreign exchange lending: they are making large speculative profits from Treasury Bills, many of which are purchased on behalf of clients using foreign currency deposit accounts (though the inflows and outflows of these accounts are ill-recorded in international statistics).

The overhang of government domestic debt is therefore discouraging any other lending (in local or foreign currency) by the banks. Other types of domestic debt — such as arrears on payments to local suppliers — discourage bank lending even more directly by branding as uncreditworthy potential clients who depend on government contracts. In addition, domestic payments arrears are a major factor taken into account by correspondent banks in assessing country creditworthiness. Bankers interviewed therefore suggested that reducing domestic debt would have a much greater effect on lending than cutting external debt.

Partly because of these distortions in the government debt market, but primarily because banking systems have historically been government-controlled or oligopolistic, a third factor which discourages banks from lending in foreign currency is the highly non-competitive nature of the banking system in many African countries, which allows banks to make huge profit margins through differentials between interest rates on local currency loans and those on local currency deposits. These differentials are also often needed by the banks to keep themselves in business, due to a large overhang of non-performing loans from the days of financial repression, and to their own inefficiency and high overheads. Differentials have ranged as high as 20-25% in our project countries, encouraging local rather than foreign currency lending. Instead it has been the clients of the banks who have been demanding foreign currency loans as they perceive the exchange rate to be stabilising and see that interest rates on foreign currency loans are much lower than those on domestic currency.

Poor performance by local banks has two other negative effects on bank lending and FDI from abroad. Local bank branches are often important sources of current and precise information on macroeconomic aspects and company performance. They also provide important services for foreign investors, notably through their lines of credit with correspondent banks. Insofar as they are unable to perform these functions effectively, investors and lenders stay away.

In spite of financial sector reform programmes in recent years, progress to healthy and competitive banking systems, and especially towards diversifying financial institutions by encouraging other organisations which could lend in foreign currency, has been slow in most of low-income Africa. A healthy banking system and a diversified financial sector are universally seen as key prerequisites for attracting new foreign bank flows.

4.5 Risk

The perception of high country risk is the most powerful factor orienting banks towards short-term secured lending. Many of the factors mentioned in Chapters 2 and 3 are influential. But bankers look upon risk in much narrower terms — as pure repayment risk rather than taking into account wider national political, economic or social conditions. As a result, virtually all medium-term lending to SSA has physical guarantees of repayment (e.g. allowing seizure of passenger and cargo aircraft or ships) or guarantees by export credit agencies, making country risk for the lender practically zero. Risk can also be reduced and shared through guarantees or cofinancing by international development finance institutions such as the World Bank, IFC, CDC and EIB. Many banks have been keen to on-lend funds provided by such institutions. These have also been combined with preferred creditor status for individual private sector lenders in various recent offshore projects, and in private sector build, operate, and transfer (BOT) infrastructure schemes such as the Maputo Corridor. Another important risk reduction factor is the involvement of a foreign or multi-national investor in a project. Many medium-term loans have been made offshore to the FDI sponsor of a project — including large South African or Zimbabwean corporations. In contrast to their smaller African counterparts, projects supported by large-scale FDI are perceived by bankers to be "viable propositions" and to have "promoters with integrity, commitment, and knowledge of what they are embarking on".

4.6 Provisioning Guidelines

Another negative factor for most international banks is the guidelines or regulations about the level of risk or loan-loss provisions they need to set aside against loans to an individual country, and the tax allowances they can receive on such provisions. Almost all countries have such guidelines. These tend to be behind the times, reflecting the economic recessions, foreign exchange shortages and restrictions, and debt reschedulings of the 1980s and early 1990s. They therefore recommend very high provisioning for countries like Tanzania, Uganda and Zambia. They also skew lending away from countries whose economies are recovering and which have freed foreign exchange flows. Because they make no allowance for recent positive circumstances, banks would have to provision heavily even against new loans. Finally, they fail to distinguish between government sovereign risk and private sector risk, discouraging lending to thriving private sector enterprises. To avoid penalising countries with strong track records, such guidelines need to be more flexible according to recent favourable economic developments and foreign exchange liberalisation, reducing or even eliminating provisions on new loans; particularly loans to the private sector ought to distinguish between sovereign and private sector risk provisioning levels. Of course, loans secured by foreign exchange proceeds or physical guarantees are exempt from such provisions. The Bank of England for example is replacing its provisioning matrix for country debt introduced in 1987, with a system where banks are responsible for presenting an assessment of their own exposure to country risk. Its matrix had become less compatible with risk-based supervision and hence less useful in assessing appropriate levels of provisions for exposure, notably to South East Asia at end 1997 (Bank of England, 1998:8; Griffith-Jones, 1998).

4.7 Export Credit and Other Guarantees

Another important barrier to new lending is that most OECD government export credit agencies (ECAs), such as the UK's Export Credit Guarantee Department, suspended guarantees against non-repayment of loans for most SSA countries in the 1980s, and have not renewed their cover since. In contrast, export credit agencies in some non-OECD countries (South Africa, India) have more generous policies for cover to SSA countries, and this is in turn an important explanation for the growth in FDI and trade with these countries.

However, the benefits of export credit guarantees for SSA economies are highly questionable. The tying of such credits to exports from the lending country can of course increase the price or reduce the quality of goods. Some OECD ECAs have been notorious for overpricing goods and corruption in their dealings with Africa. It should be remembered that many unguaranteed loans also lack transparency, with banks or exporters relying on single sources of goods (EFA 1996; 1993). The most negative aspect of export credit guarantees is therefore the frequent involvement of SSA governments in having to explicitly or implicitly guarantee payment by the private sector, with potential high costs for the budget if private sector borrowers default. Recent initiatives to provide debt relief (particularly for Heavily Indebted Poor Countries such as Tanzania, Uganda and Zambia) have been accompanied by pledges to expand new export credits — but these should be carefully restricted to private sector loans with no government guarantees, or there will be a strong risk that HIPC country debts will rapidly become unpayable again.

4.8 External Debt Burden

Large external debt stocks owed by SSA countries have deterred new lending. An important question is to what extent reductions in SSA commercial debt, for example via buy back operations, have improved those countries' creditworthiness, and their access to new bank lending. Our interviews and those carried out by London Economics (1996) show that in SSA unlike Latin America, the effect of commercial debt reduction on creditworthiness has been marginal, although it has brought other benefits. This is largely because commercial debt is a relatively small proportion of total. There were strong mixed feelings regarding the Zambia buyback of 1994 for example. Most bankers felt banks and investors had forgotten it so it had no effect on lending. But some felt that it left a bad aftertaste with banks and particularly businesses that had been involved in the country over a long period, and thereby discouraged new flows. Thus reduction of the commercial debt overhang has not led to new flows.

New flows will be more likely if and when SSA finally obtains sufficient relief on its overall debt to make its servicing sustainable and compatible with economic growth, as is explained under the HIPC Initiative. Indeed, a recent study (Bhattacharya, Montiel and Sharma, 1996) provides clear econometric evidence that for 1980-95, SSA countries with a lower external debt burden have attracted significantly more private lending. In addition Uganda's experience shows that where debt ratios are falling due to growth and debt reduction, commercial lending is resuming. This is therefore a crucial step, but it should be remembered that Africa's access to bank credit was relatively limited (though improving) even before the

1980s debt crisis. Though the debt problems made the situation worse, reducing the overall debt overhang might therefore have a less dramatic impact on access to new flows than in Latin America.

It is also worth stressing that even in Latin America commercial debt reduction did not lead to a major return of bank lending. Rather, other flows such as FDI and especially portfolio flows picked up significantly as the debt overhang was reduced, and general economic prospects were seen to improve in the early 1990s. Recent rises in private flows to Uganda show a similar pattern. Further, when bank lending to Latin America resumed in the early and mid-90s, it was led mainly by European banks which had lent relatively little in the 1970s and early 1980s, and had thus suffered far smaller losses from the debt crisis. Given the strong presence of European banks in Africa, this might augur more positively for resumption of bank flows. More importantly, as discussed above, South African and also Asian banks are starting to lend. They do not have a history of debt overhang which makes it easier for them to start.

Some have suggested that one possible way to improve the link between debt reduction and new flows for SSA may be via greater expansion of debt equity swaps, not just for commercial but also for bilateral official debt (Mistry and Griffith-Jones, 1993). In the early 1990s this seemed a particularly attractive vehicle for facilitating privatisation. However, the scale of debt reduction planned under the HIPC Initiative (up to 80%) may sharply reduce the scope for investors to gain subsidies from the margin between the reduction percentage and the secondary market price, reducing the attractiveness of such deals to both investors and governments.

Chapter 5 Credit Ratings

Nils Bhinda, Stephany Griffith-Jones and Matthew Martin

The views of credit ratings agencies are one key input in international capital market perception of Africa. Credit ratings are a crucial determinant of whether — and on what terms — countries are able to issue bonds on international markets. Indeed, the absence of credit ratings for most African countries helps to explain why so few countries have issued international bonds. Rating agencies also claim to have a major influence on multinationals, banks, professional investors, and fund managers, with many "building in ratings as a mandatory part of the decision process".

The ratings agencies fall into two categories. The credit ratings given by formal agencies (IBCA, Standard & Poors, Moody's) have a direct impact on bond prices, the success of a bond launch, and on mutual funds. The ratings given by other agencies (such as the Economist Intelligence Unit, Institutional Investor, Euromoney) provide information investors read occasionally and sometimes, usually informally, factor into their investment decisions.

This chapter examines ratings in four ways, by looking at their country coverage, methodology, results for SSA as a whole, and for our project countries. It shows that most are highly subjective, in spite of seemingly scientific methodologies. Further, while they show that the climate for capital flows to SSA has been improving, they lag far behind actual improvements (or problems), and their country coverage and methodology produce clear biases against Sub-Saharan Africa.

5.1 Country Coverage

The countries covered in the ratings vary dramatically. Of the informal agencies, Euromoney (EM) rates 180, Institutional Investor (II) 135, and Economist Intelligence Unit (EIU) 100 countries. EM covers the most Sub-Saharan countries (44), followed by II (29) and EIU (17). SSA is even more poorly represented by the formal agencies: Standard & Poors and IBCA rate only South Africa; Moody's adds Mauritius.

The formal agencies ascribe this above all to limited staff resources. They suggest that the informal agencies have a less rigorous evaluation process, and other sources (a panel of experts for EM and II, and a full country risk analysis service for EIU). The informal agencies also blame lack of data or interest among the investor community.

Other reasons often given are less plausible. The first is that "few SSA countries have economic performance worthy of a rating": but this view is inconsistent with the views of the informal agencies and other analysts in the international financial community, who rate performance of Botswana, Mauritius and Namibia level with or above South Africa.

The second is that "countries do not approach formal agencies" (normally the first step to a rating) because they are not issuing bonds: but the reality is that most SSA countries do not answer initial approaches from agencies, because they are discouraged by their low existing rating, or have no chance of an investment grade rating which would allow them to issue a bond. Some ratings staff suggest a lower rating is worthwhile, to signal improving policy to the market, and to encourage governments to "maintain good behaviour to keep their rating". But most commercial analysts believe a country should ask for rating only if it will get an investment grade: a lower rating will attract only expensive, short-term capital and diminish prospects for medium-term loans or bonds.

5.2 Methodology

5.2.1 Institutional Investor

II surveys 75-100 of the world's largest commercial banks, and weights them according to their worldwide exposure and the sophistication of their country analysis. But it has no clearly defined methodology, causing large biases and inconsistencies. II has written that its results "must be seen as arithmetical averages and not as evidence of consensus" due to "widespread and interesting differences in the scores each respondent gives to various countries" (September 1993). These wide spreads (which are more pronounced for the lower-ranked countries) make arithmetical averages inaccurate and misleading: presenting the range of scores would be more informative.

These spring from a complex mix of factors, most of which penalise Sub-Saharan Africa. Poor information (which applies particularly to low-income countries) is the most important. II explained the wide spread of views on Malawi by saying: "how much does any lender know, or bother to find out, about Malawi before rating it?". Many other SSA countries are similarly written off. Familiarity with one's neighbours is also central: Western Europeans rate Eastern Europe highly, and Singaporean bankers favour Vietnam. South African bankers support African countries — but there are far fewer South African members in the survey sample. Non-

Western bankers also tend to be more optimistic about developing countries (Asian bankers rated Mexico in 1996 higher than North Americans) but are under-represented. Finally, continuing business ties lead French banks to look favourably on Francophone Africa, and Portuguese banks on Angola and Mozambique. As discussed in the previous chapter, many Western banks have been reducing their operations in Africa.

All four factors lead to a negative subjective bias against Sub-Saharan Africa, making II's survey unresponsive to positive economic and political events. II's results are indicative of long-term perceptions — indeed of unchanging prejudices. They can be overcome only by improving information flows to those surveyed, and diversifying the survey sample by increasing the representation of non-Western bankers and key regional players.

5.2.2 Euromoney

Based on assessments by 45 political risk specialists and economists at major financial institutions, EM's survey appears more scientific and objective than II's, with clearly defined and weighted criteria, and quoted data and information sources. On closer inspection however, there is a high element of subjectivity and judgment in EM's evaluation of economic performance and political risk. Economic performance (which has a 25% weighting) is based on 2-year projections made by EM. These often change sharply over a very short period, indicating that they are based more on perceived than actual recent economic performance. Political risk (25%), based on responses from risk analysts, is highly subjective and difficult to quantify.

The other criteria used also contain large subjective elements, which tend to work against developing countries. An average of formal credit rating scores absorbs 10% (but these have their own biases — and countries score zero if they are not rated); 5% is forfaiting data from banks; and 5% is availability of export credit agency cover for short-term finance. Many apparently objective "economic data" categories also work in biassed ways: for example, OECD countries not reporting to the World Bank are automatically granted full marks for "debt indicators" and "access to bank finance", but non-reporting developing countries score zero. If formal rating agencies, banks, export credit agencies and the World Bank were more open-minded and comprehensive in their coverage, most Sub-Saharan and least developed countries would score much higher. For those who do not read tables, the accompanying textual analysis barely mentions SSA except for South Africa, reinforcing the negative impression that SSA is not worth analysing.

Overall, EM's survey is the most volatile. This reflects not dramatic changes in economic fundamentals, but dramatically changing interpretation by analysts of short-term changes in economic data.

5.2.3 Economist Intelligence Unit

Prior to 1997, EIU's ratings were subject to some of the same criticisms as Institutional Investor. Large proportions of their ratings scores were determined subjectively, and the overall scoring system caused biases because it worked in increments of 5/100. This meant that for 7 criteria which each have a 5% weighting, a country could only score 5 or 0. So a country marginally above average could receive 5 marks, while one marginally below average could receive 0. This exaggerated the gap between rich and poor countries, and ignored improvements in performance from a low level. It also exaggerated peaks and troughs in cycles of political or economic uncertainty. EIU exacerbated this inflexibility in tracking improvements in performance by dividing countries arbitrarily into 5 broad bands of creditworthiness, making changes in category rare.

However, EIU now produces the best informed, most objective results, based on staff assessments and a detailed database and written analysis for each country. As a result of a change in methodology in 1997, there is little to criticise in their methodology. Firstly, it assesses political risk, economic policy risk, economic structure risk and liquidity risk. Virtually all of these different risk categories are measured using objective economic data (the exception being some elements of political risk), implying that over 75% of the assessment is not vulnerable to accusations of subjectivity.

Secondly, and in marked contrast to the other informal agencies, EIU now distinguishes different degrees of risk for the different types of capital flows an investor might be considering (currency risk, sovereign debt risk and banking sector risk). Thirdly, because of its extensive supporting analysis and databases, updated every quarter, EIU's data are more current and their analysis better informed than the other agencies.

5.3 How Does SSA Fare and Why?

Of the 29 SSA countries rated by II, 26 score well below the global average, and 20 are among the 30 lowest countries. EM rates the same three 3 countries above average (South Africa, Botswana and Mauritius), and the rest well behind. Nearly half its bottom 90 are from SSA. EIU also ranks Africa lower than European and Asian countries (see also Haque *et al*, 1996), but in general many SSA countries are ranked higher by EIU than the other two agencies.

What explains these results? First, individual country ratings are lowered by negative perceptions of regional political, economic, and social factors. SSA has a reputation for political instability, which penalises all countries in the more subjective ratings. Thus, while individual ratings and the SSA average have been rising over time in EM and II surveys, SSA lags behind and is expected to stay there. Its "modest gains" are rarely more than a reflection of "a generalised optimism" about emerging markets. "You know banks are feeling better when Africa goes up" said one banker.

Second, econometric analysis of the ratings of EIU and II since 1980 and EM since 1982 by Haque *et al* (1996) has important lessons. This study is based on analysis of economic determinants in these ratings for over 60 developing countries, running regressions to assess the persistence of ratings for countries over time, country-specific factors, and external variables. Regressions results show that:

- ratings are influenced by export composition. "In EM and II ratings regressions, all other country groupings appear to have significantly lower rankings than the exporters of manufactured goods" and "the EIU appears to attach significantly negative ratings to only fuel exporters and producers of primary products" (Haque *et al*, 1996:28). All have lower rankings for countries dependent on a single export. This may be justifiable as commodity export prices are more volatile, and tend to decline relative to manufactured goods, but relegates most SSA countries. Analysis of the study suggests this may be the case, with South Africa and Zimbabwe (with broader manufacturing and export bases) rated more highly than Uganda and Zambia (dependent until recently on coffee and copper).

- all developing countries lose from high international interest rates in all ratings, regardless of domestic economic developments. This is well-known to market analysts — emerging markets always suffer when OECD interests offer higher returns.

Third, countries get stuck in arbitrary groups, which lead agencies to react only very slowly (if at all) to significant changes in policy or outcomes. Agencies vary in the value they give to the stability of their ratings. EM prides itself on tracking the global economic upturn and improved creditworthiness of the late 1980s much more rapidly than its competitors. On the other hand, Standard and Poors prefers to review ratings only once a year, "to come up with a stable rating".

There is little doubt that investors and African countries prefer stable ratings only if they reflect stable country policies and creditworthiness: ratings should reflect country conditions as they change, not inflexible rating systems or outdated information.

5.4 Project Country Observations

To assess the factors influencing African ratings more closely, we looked in more detail at informal ratings of our project countries, .for which we had excellent information sources.

II's and EIU's relative rankings for our project countries are the same over time, whereas those for EM change more sharply (Tables 5.1a-c). South Africa has been top in all three, followed by Zimbabwe, with the other three countries well behind (less so according to EM). In general, EM was more positive about our project countries, followed by EIU and II, until 1997, while EIU's ratings have risen sharply since 1997 (Figures 5.1a-e). Referring back to our earlier discussion of methodology, this indicates that the more subjective the ratings, the lower SSA countries are rated, though greater objectivity and more frequent data collection may cause more volatile ratings.

It is also possible to see two notable lags in measurement of changing performance, for Uganda and Zimbabwe. It took 8 years of adjustment and 10 years of political stability before Uganda's rating rose sharply. The eventual rise reflected sharp increases in objective economic performance, partly due to the coffee boom of the mid-1990s, with indicators of political risk (and therefore the agencies depending on them) lagging behind. As late as 1994, II ranked Uganda last in its survey and described it as "destined to remain...(with)...the likes of...Zaire and Haiti". Even after this rise, it ranked until September 1996 below Tanzania and Zambia according to

Table 5.1a Institutional Investor's Sovereign Ratings and Ranking for Project Countries, (1992-98)

	3/92	9/92	3/93	9/93	3/94	9/94	3/95	9/95	3/96	9/96	3/97	9/97	3/98	9/98
South Africa	39.3	39.8	39.8	38.2	38.9	40	42.5	45.2	46.3	46.3	46	46.4	46.5	46.6
	45	*44*	*45*	*50*	*51*	*52*	*50*	*47*	*46*	*48*	*51*	*51*	*50*	*48*
Tanzania	12.5	11.8	12.9	14	13.9	15.2	15.5	16.7	17.7	18.1	18.1	18.7	19.3	19.9
	103	*110*	*110*	*111*	*113*	*111*	*110*	*108*	*104*	*106*	*105*	*110*	*110*	*106*
Uganda	5.5	5.2	7.3	8.4	10.1	11.6	12.9	13.1	14.5	16.1	17.7	20.1	21.2	19.9
	119	*126*	*121*	*123*	*122*	*121*	*119*	*119*	*117*	*113*	*107*	*103*	*104*	*107*
Zambia	9.8	9.5	11.7	12.4	13.1	13.9	14.6	15.1	15.7	16.5	16.1	16	17.5	17.2
	106	*113*	*112*	*116*	*115*	*116*	*115*	*115*	*111*	*112*	*113*	*115*	*113*	*114*
Zimbabwe	28.3	26.1	27.7	26.9	27.9	29	30.7	31	32.2	32.5	32.3	33.8	33.6	29.8
	61	*65*	*66*	*70*	*68*	*70*	*67*	*66*	*65*	*68*	*71*	*68*	*73*	*82*

Notes:
Italicised information denotes global rank.
Institutional Investor grades country risk on a scale of 1-100: 100 being entirely risk free, 0 being the worst.

Table 5.1b Euromoney's Sovereign Ratings and Ranking for Project Countries (1992-98)*

	9/92	3/93	9/93	3/94	9/94	3/95	9/95	3/96	9/96	3/97	9/97	9/98
South Africa	53.90	59.04	60.04	60.25	58.96	62.86	63.56	64.86	62.30	69.88	67.83	61.09
	47	*43*	*49*	*45*	*48*	*45*	*46*	*49*	*48*	*48*	*44*	*50*
Tanzania	19.31	22.68	25.15	27.47	31.89	29.58	27.57	32.34	29.52	28.49	32.59	36.14
	137	*130*	*135*	*133*	*117*	*133*	*140*	*125*	*136*	*139*	*115*	*120*
Uganda	22.34	21.06	24.22	31.14	31.39	28.40	24.74	41.70	37.65	36.70	36.94	43.00
	127	*135*	*140*	*120*	*120*	*139*	*150*	*96*	*99*	*105*	*100*	*91*
Zambia	17.68	20.29	24.91	25.96	26.23	28.56	28.54	34.81	32.76	21.84	24.03	32.84
	147	*141*	*136*	*139*	*133*	*138*	*135*	*113*	*120*	*157*	*148*	*136*
Zimbabwe	42.67	44.78	45.02	42.69	44.95	50.13	49.41	50.49	46.14	42.00	40.88	43.22
	59	*57*	*69*	*77*	*74*	*63*	*66*	*71*	*76*	*95*	*91*	*90*

Notes:
* No surveys were conducted in March 1992 or March 1998.
Italicised information denotes global rank.
Euromoney grades country risk on a scale of 1-100: 100 being entirely risk free, 0 being the worst.

Table 5.1c Economist Intelligence Unit's Sovereign Ratings for Project Countries (1992-98)*

	3/92	9/92	3/93	9/93	3/94	9/94	3/95	9/95	3/96	9/96	3/97	9/97	3/98	9/98
South Africa	55	50	50	50	50	55	60	60	60	60	49	52	50	48
	C	*C*	*C*	*C*	*C*	*B*	*B*	*B*	*B*	*B*	*C*	*C*	*C*	*C*
Tanzania	-	-	-	-	-	-	-	-	-	30	37	37	38	39
	-	-	-	-	-	-	-	-	-	*D*	*D*	*D*	*D*	*D*
Uganda	-	-	-	-	-	-	-	-	-	-	-	-	-	43
	-	-	-	-	-	-	-	-	-	-	-	-	-	*C*
Zambia	20	20	20	20	20	20	20	20	25	20	30	28	30	27
	E	*E*	*E*	*E*	*E*	*E*	*E*	*E*	*D*	*E*	*D*	*D*	*D*	*D*
Zimbabwe	40	35	30	35	40	40	50	50	50	50	47	43	37	32
	D	*D*	*D*	*D*	*D*	*D*	*C*	*C*	*C*	*C*	*C*	*C*	*C*	*D*

Notes:
* EIU publishes ratings quarterly, but for ease of comparison with other raters, and as they are highly stable over time, we use only the March and September surveys. Methodology changed in January 1997.
Italicised information denotes global category, as defined in the methodology. No information is as yet available to us on EIU's global rankings.
EIU grades country risk on a scale of 1-100: 0 being entirely risk free, 100 being the worst. For sake of comparison with the other raters, we have reversed this scale, by subtracting EIU's rating from 100.

II, though it has leapfrogged them according to EM a full year earlier (Figures 5.2a-b). On the other hand, no rating agency noticed the gradual economic decline in Zimbabwe until 1997-98.

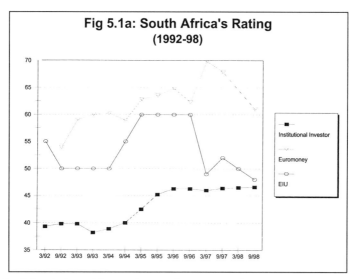

Fig 5.1a: South Africa's Rating (1992-98)

Methodological problems also explain some sharp changes. For example, Zambia rose 22 places in 1995-98 according to EM, due to favourable economic performance and improved forfaiting terms, but this improvement was not noticed by any other agency.

All of the lower-ranked countries were affected by an upward global trend in emerging market confidence in the early 1990s, which has now been largely reversed.

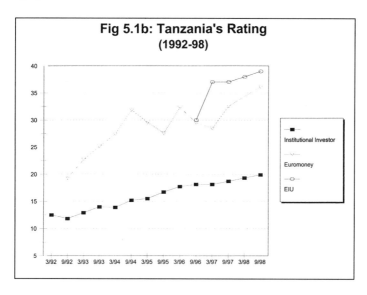

Fig 5.1b: Tanzania's Rating (1992-98)

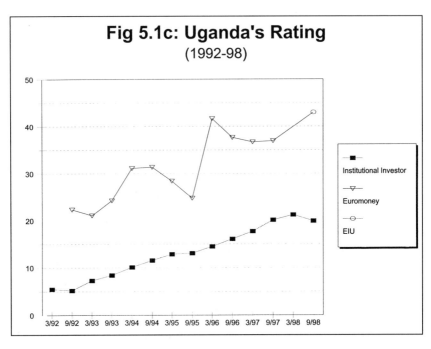

Fig 5.1c: Uganda's Rating
(1992-98)

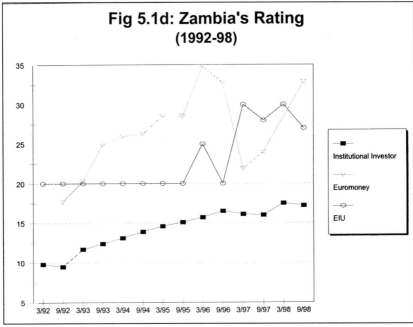

Fig 5.1d: Zambia's Rating
(1992-98)

Fig 5.1e: Zimbabwe's Rating
(1992-98)

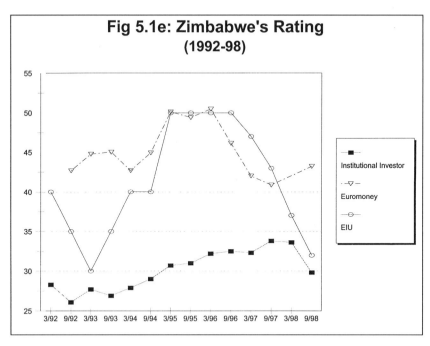

Fig 5.2a: Institutional Investor Ranks
(Percentile of Sample, 3/92- 3/97)

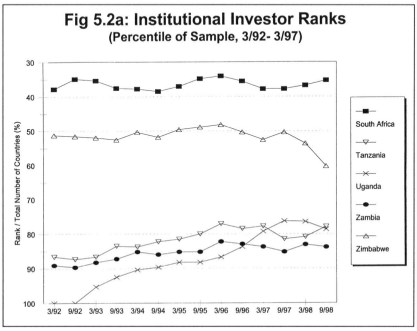

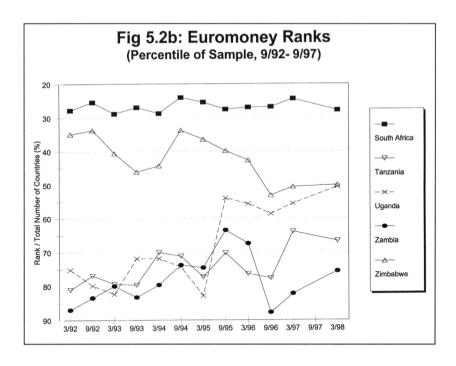

Fig 5.2b: Euromoney Ranks
(Percentile of Sample, 9/92- 9/97)

Legend:
- ■— South Africa
- —▽— Tanzania
- —✕— Uganda
- ●— Zambia
- —△— Zimbabwe

5.5 Conclusions

This chapter has shown that the methodology of ratings depends too much on subjective perception and outdated data. Together with their limited country coverage, these factors automatically bias ratings against most African (and other low-income) countries.

Rating agencies acknowledge that many criteria are subjective, and that others which appear objective contain large subjective components. Some ratings agencies (notably EIU) have made major efforts to improve their methodology. Agencies also argue that the elements of subjective perception match the views of those considering investments, but this in turn reflects a narrow view: they share and therefore reinforce the negative perceptions of those global investors who are less likely to invest, but do not sufficiently reflect the views of analysts or intra-regional investors. As a result, global investors are missing out on important investment opportunities.

Fortunately, it does not appear that ratings are the crucial determinants of most investment decisions. They were not cited by our survey respondents as important for any type of flow except bonds — which means that they are irrelevant to private capital flows for most SSA countries. But, as

Sub-Saharan Africa becomes increasingly integrated into global financial markets, it will be essential that rating agencies expand their country coverage and improve their methodology to reflect the true investment climate of the continent.

Further, a recent study (Merchant International Group, 1999) showed that there are a host of hidden and non-conventional risks, or "grey area dynamics", that can cause assets to underperform. These include crime, fraud, business cronyism, and local customs and attitudes. Investors lose out simply because they pay too little attention to them, and similarly, these tend to be overlooked in the risk assessments of rating agencies and banks.

Part 3

Reality: The Impact of Capital Flows and Policy Responses

Chapter 6 Macroeconomic Impact

Jonathan Leape

Private capital flows have had pervasive effects on African economies in the 1990s. While all five countries in this study benefited from the world-wide surge in private capital flows to developing countries in this period, the timing of the rise in flows, especially of their macroeconomic impact, was most closely linked to internal developments. In particular, it was the acceleration of the process of financial sector reform and the liberalisation of exchange controls that were in all countries the most decisive factors.

The concerted programmes of liberalisation and reform were a decisive factor in stimulating new private capital inflows. International investors responded to the increasingly credible signals of government commitment to more market-oriented policies and to maintaining an investor-friendly environment. Also important — most obviously in the East African countries — was the return of flight capital, attracted by the reforms.

The reforms also, however, heightened the macroeconomic impact of private capital movements. By freeing key prices in the economies — most importantly the exchange rate and interest rates — the reforms created a set of transmission mechanisms through which changes in cross-border capital flows had important real and monetary effects on the economies. Although the microeconomic foundations for these macroeconomic effects are beyond the scope of this study, the macroeconomic effects of capital flows have been amplified by rigidities in these economies arising from incomplete markets (such as bond and stock markets); underdeveloped sectors (such as small and medium-scale enterprises); and high transaction and information costs. It is the presence of such rigidities that underlies "gap" theories, which postulate that capital inflows can enable developing countries to achieve higher rates of economic growth by helping to bridge foreign exchange or savings or absorptive capacity gaps.

The most important macroeconomic effects are evident first in the balance of payments, second in savings, investment and growth, and third in monetary policy and financial markets.

6.1 Balance of Payments

For much of Africa, the balance of payments has long been driven by developments affecting the current account. Most important have been swings in world commodity prices. Primary products account for a dominant share of exports throughout Africa, and this is evident in the five countries examined in this study. In Uganda, for example, coffee accounted for almost 60 percent of goods exported in 1997. A similar dependence on primary goods is evident in Tanzania and Zimbabwe, although Tanzania is less dependent on a single crop than Uganda and Zimbabwe has a relatively diversified primary sector. The dependence is most striking in Zambia, where the copper producer ZCCM generates more than 90% of export earnings. Even in South Africa, with its more developed manufacturing base, net gold exports accounted for almost 20% in 1997.

However, the current account has been less of a driving force in the 1990s. The sharp rise in private capital flows in all five countries has had a significant impact on the balance of payments. This impact is evident in exchange rates (see Figures 6.1a-e), and on reserves, imports and exports.

Private capital flows have had significant effects on nominal and real exchange rates since the beginning of the 1990s. Through the 1980s, dependence on mineral and other primary exports combined, in most cases, with a large external debt led to persistent overvaluation of the exchange rate — a problem that was exacerbated by fixed exchange rate policies. This led, in turn, to the development of parallel foreign exchange markets and, frequently, a multiplicity of exchange rates. In this environment, changes in the balance of payments were not reflected in the rigid official exchange rate, but did rapidly affect the parallel market premium.

The liberalisation of foreign exchange markets eliminated parallel markets in the first half of the 1990s. Unification of the foreign exchange market has

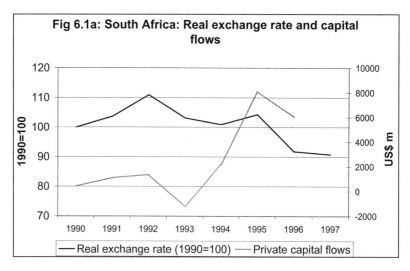

Fig 6.1a: South Africa: Real exchange rate and capital flows

— Real exchange rate (1990=100) —— Private capital flows

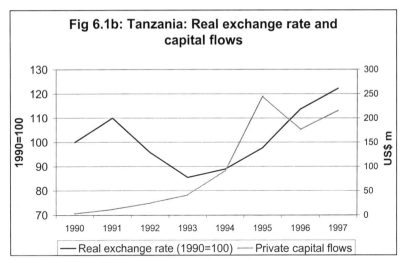

Fig 6.1b: Tanzania: Real exchange rate and capital flows

— Real exchange rate (1990=100) —— Private capital flows

made rates more volatile — even where the previous official exchange rate was already fully floating. Some of this volatility is a verification of the volatility that was previously confined to parallel markets, but much of it stems from the greater volume and volatility of the private capital flows in all countries.

In Tanzania, Uganda and Zambia, the liberalisation of the foreign exchange market — which started with efforts to begin liberalising the current account in the first half of the 1980s — rapidly gathered pace in the early 1990s following sharp depreciations of the exchange rate. Although the timing of the depreciations varied, the precipitating factor in each case

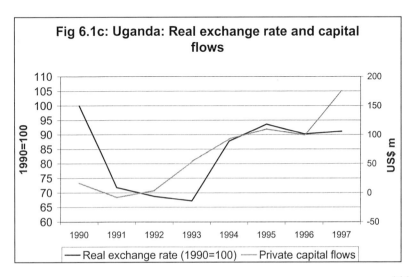

Fig 6.1c: Uganda: Real exchange rate and capital flows

— Real exchange rate (1990=100) —— Private capital flows

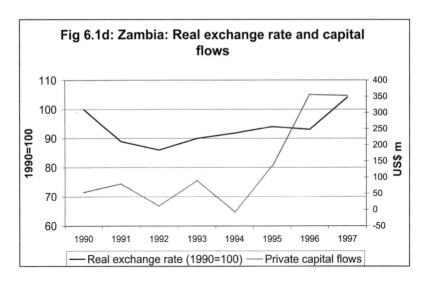

Fig 6.1d: Zambia: Real exchange rate and capital flows

— Real exchange rate (1990=100) — Private capital flows

was the interaction of financial liberalisation and a large repressed demand for foreign exchange. This was driven by a history of low foreign and domestic investor confidence, which had been associated with financial indiscipline and macroeconomic instability, as evident in fiscal deficits and inflation rates. The initial reaction to liberalisation was therefore large-scale capital flight.

However, the sharp depreciation gave new impetus to the reform pro-

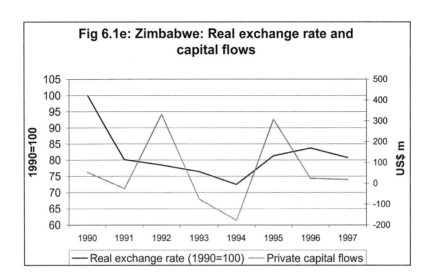

Fig 6.1e: Zimbabwe: Real exchange rate and capital flows

— Real exchange rate (1990=100) — Private capital flows

cess and led to rapid moves in the direction of liberalisation. In Tanzania, for example, the government enacted a series of reforms in February 1992. It created a second "window" for foreign exchange by allowing the establishment of private foreign exchange bureaux, freed the holding of foreign exchange by residents and eased procedures for foreign exchange receipts and payments. In Uganda, a string of reforms culminated in November 1993, when the introduction of the interbank foreign exchange market completed the transition to a unified foreign exchange market.

Having liberalised current account transactions by 1993, the project countries proceeded to liberalise the capital account but, as discussed in Chapter 7, using sharply divergent strategies.

With these reforms to the current and then capital account came a determination to allow the exchange rate to adjust to changing market conditions. All countries adopted floating exchange rate regimes, accompanied by increasingly flexible and market-sensitive strategies for intervention, as discussed below.

These regimes have made the exchange rate more sensitive to shifts in capital flows — but through the real more than the nominal exchange rate. Figures 6.1a-e show the annual changes in private capital flows and the real exchange rate in the five countries. While experience varies across countries, there are clear periods when capital flows had significant effects on the real exchange rate. One example is South Africa in 1995. Following heavy capital outflows in early 1994, South Africa experienced a surge in capital inflows following the successful democratic elections in April. The real exchange rate, which fell slightly in 1994, increased significantly in 1995.

There has also been a positive relationship between inflows and the nominal exchange rate in Zimbabwe from 1990, and especially after 1994 when the authorities adopted a floating rate. Strong capital inflows in the first half of 1994 led to an appreciation of almost 6% in the nominal exchange rate; in the second half of the year capital outflows led to a 3% depreciation. The Zimbabwean experience illustrates a complication in assessing the impact of capital inflows on the exchange rate, and the balance of payments more generally: namely, the difficulty of assessing the relative impact of private and official capital flows. In Zimbabwe, as in all the other countries except South Africa, balance of payments support has been an important component of donor assistance. Thus, the authorities' ability to intervene in the foreign exchange market to influence the exchange rate is related most directly to official, rather than private, capital inflows. For this reason, the level of official flows may have, or be perceived to have, a more direct impact on the exchange rate than private flows. On the other hand, the lower volatility of official flows may work in the opposite direction (Kufeni *et al*, 1997). In any event, evidence suggests that Zimbabwe's exchange rate stability and liberalisation in the early 1990s were dependent on strong private inflows. The subsequent loss of most of its balance of payments support in the mid-1990s has pushed authorities to the point of confiscating private flows to attempt to intervene on the exchange rate.

The experiences of Tanzania and Uganda in 1994-5 provide further examples of the impact of private capital flows on the real exchange rate. Both countries experienced sharp rises in capital inflows and the real exchange rate in 1994 and 1995. However, they also illustrate another intervening factor. Coffee is the principal export of both countries and, during 1994-5, there was an increase in world market prices of 15%. This price boom led to a sharp rise in export earnings and in capital flows. The change in the terms of trade was critical to the appreciation of the real exchange rate. The link between the terms of trade and capital inflows is also evident in Zambia, where there is a strong correlation between traditional exports and FDI as well as net short-term debt.

Nevertheless, it is possible due to the segmentation of markets to identify clear effects of private capital flows on the exchange rate in both Tanzania and Uganda. In both countries, large amounts of private capital flows have flowed through the bureaux market, which has been the benchmark for the foreign exchange market in most of the 1990s. The bulk of flows through this market were not export proceeds but private flows. Moreover, even the repatriation of export proceeds represents in a sense private flows: until recent years, they would have been kept outside the country or under-reported. For Tanzania, statistical tests taking into account changes in the terms of trade have found a strong effect on the real exchange rate of changes in private capital flows. Using the long-term concept of the real equilibrium exchange rate (REER) and data for the period 1968 to 1995, the results in Kimei *et al* (1997) suggest that a (permanent) 1% increase in net capital inflows may lead to an appreciation of 4%.

Private capital flows can also have a direct impact on exports and imports. The effects on exports have, in general, been minimal. While authorities acknowledge the desirability of FDI in the export sector, such investment has been small — especially in non-traditional products. In Zambia, for example, there is a strong positive relationship between capital inflows, especially FDI, and traditional exports (copper, cobalt, zinc), but not with non-traditional exports (agricultural products, processed food, semi-precious stones, engineering products). This suggests that private flows, including FDI have so far not been sufficiently aimed towards this sub-sector (Matale *et al*, 1997:52). Too often, inward investment is instead

114

aimed at producing consumer durables, such as luxury cars, for the domestic market. There have, however, been some exceptions to this pattern, such as the cut flower industry in Zimbabwe.

Generally, private flows and imports have had a strong positive relationship. This has been unambiguous in Tanzania (Kimei et al, 1997) and Uganda, where imports have increased substantially as a result of FDI and private transfers (Kasekende et al, 1997:27, 28), and in Zimbabwe with total imports almost doubling from $1.3bn in 1989 to $2.2bn in 1996 (Kufeni et al, 1997:3) against a background of sharply higher private capital inflows. Zambian tests found links only between FDI and related capital goods imports — data were unavailable to test the anticipated effects of short-term suppliers lines of credit (Matale et al, 1997:49).

The effects on imports are one of the important transmission mechanisms via which capital flows influence economic development and growth. In all of these countries, the balance of payments has long been a constraint on growth. As small open economies with relatively high import intensities, a significant increase in the rate of growth tends to induce a sharp rise in imports. This mechanism is particularly important in South Africa, where increases in fixed investment have strong effects on import levels due to the large imported component of investments in capital equipment and machinery (Khatri et al, 1997).

This mechanism has also contributed in South Africa to an inverse relationship between the current account balance and capital movements. A rise in economic activity has tended to drive the current account into deficit — due to the increase in imports, and the tendency of exporters to switch back to the local market when demand is sufficiently high. At the same time, higher imports are usually associated with greater use of foreign trade finance. This positive effect on the capital account is typically reinforced by the higher interest rates that result as liquidity conditions tighten. Higher rates further increase capital inflows as importers and exporters switch from domestic to offshore sources of trade finance, domestic companies turn to foreign finance for new investments and foreign investors are attracted by higher rates of return (Khatri et al, 1997).

Overall, the existence of a positive correlation between terms of trade changes and capital inflows can lead to strong boom and bust cycles —for example in Tanzania and Uganda in 1994-95 (Kimei et al, 1997:32; Kasekende et al, 1997). The result has been pronounced volatility in the overall balance of payments and the economy more generally, with important implications for macroeconomic management, as discussed in Chapter 7. Capital flows have, however, been largely counter-cyclical — inversely correlated with terms of trade — in South Africa (Khatri et al, 1997:3- 13). The same pattern is evident in Zimbabwe, where high export demand has resulted in higher inflows, especially of short-term bank loans. This effect is strengthened due to Zimbabwe's "relatively thin capital and financial markets, which have been characterised by a high cost of borrowing, hence making cheaper foreign credit lines more attractive" (Kufeni et al, 1997:47-8).

The effect of private capital flows on foreign exchange reserves has been mixed and variable across countries. Official and private flows combined have had a strong positive effect on reserves in Tanzania and Uganda. It is difficult to disaggregate the relative importance of each, but the increase in FDI is believed to have been the key factor in Tanzania (Kimei et al, 1997:30), whereas the Ugandans see donor flows as central (Kasekende et al, 1997:28). In Zimbabwe, however, private capital flows have certainly influenced reserves, though the relationship broke down in 1991-3 (Kufeni et al, 1997:50-51). In South Africa, this effect has varied over time. In the 1960s and 1970s, it was typically muted, due to the inverse relationship between the current account balance and net capital flows. In recent years, however, it has been strong and positive, with periods of capital inflows since 1994 being characterised by sharp rises in foreign reserves (Khatri et al, 1997:3-5).

In all countries, the effects of capital flows on the exchange rate and the level of reserves are heavily influenced by the authorities' intervention strategies in the foreign exchange market, as discussed in Chapter 7. In Tanzania, Uganda and Zambia, the less developed state of money and capital markets has severely circumscribed the scope for sterilisation of capital flows, particularly because establishing and maintaining macroeconomic stability is the overriding objective of economic policy. This leads to relatively greater pressure to appreciate the exchange rate in order to adjust to capital flows. While governments would like to vary their policy response according to how investment-oriented and irreversible capital flows are perceived to be, such information is not available. In this light, macroeconomic stability takes precedence over concerns about decreasing competitiveness.

For all countries except South Africa, the result — as evident in Figures 6.1a-e — has been a significant rise in the real exchange rate over the period 1993 to 1997. Kasekende et al (1997:29) estimate that in Uganda the real exchange rate appreciated by more than 11% between 1994 and 1997. In Tanzania, Kimei et al (1997:43) estimate that the exchange rate became overvalued from 1994, with the cumulative overvaluation reaching about 20% by the end of 1996.

6.2 Savings, Investment and Growth

The second important set of effects has been on the level of savings and investment. While the evidence available from the project countries suggests some tentative findings with respect to investment and growth, relatively little can be said about the effects on savings.

This is, in part, the result of weaknesses in the economic analysis of savings, whose macroeconomic determinants continue to be poorly understood. But it is mainly a product of the weakness of available data. Savings statistics in national accounts data are typically residuals, and thus are subject to the cumulative effect of measurement errors in consumer expenditure and income. The problem is, of course, worse when these errors are large, as we would expect in the less developed countries that are the focus of this study.

In most countries, the data suggest that capital inflows have supplemented domestic savings (e.g. Khatri et al, 1997:3-11), but no clear pattern emerges from the studies on the positive or negative impacts of capital flows on savings. Tanzania finds a negative correlation between FDI and domestic savings since 1991 (Kimei et al, 1997:25-6). Zambia finds a positive correlation between FDI and private consumption, although the direct correlation with domestic savings is insignificant (Matale et al, 1997:50-1). However, the findings of Kasekende et al (1997:32) for Uganda are likely to hold for most of the region. They find it impossible to identify the impact of capital flows on domestic savings, as it is swamped by the negative effects on savings of extremely high inflation and a weak financial system and, more recently, by the positive effects of public sector savings. The switch in 1992/3 from fiscal deficits to fiscal surpluses has contributed to a rise in gross national savings from 0.3% of GDP in 1991/2 to 7.6% in 1995/6. The effects on savings of these factors — inflation, financial sector development and, especially, public sector savings — have in every country dominated the effects of private flows.

By contrast, the impact of capital flows on investment has been consistently positive, although varying considerably in degree. In Tanzania, the effect on gross fixed capital formation has been positive, but weak, since 1991: but available data are not sufficient to distinguish these effects from those of other factors including the National Investment Protection and Promotion Act (1991), increased political stability, the successful privatisation programme, export retention schemes for foreign exchange, own-funded imports, and a conducive exchange rate regime (Kimei et al, 1997:26-7).

In Uganda, significant growth in private investment as a share of GDP in part reflects the surge in private capital inflows and transfers. The growth in sectors such as manufacturing and construction suggests that a significant fraction of inflows have been used to finance investment rather than consumption. Official inflows have also been an important influence (Kasekende *et al*, 1997:32-3).

In Zambia, gross domestic investment is positively correlated with FDI. Although it was not possible to disaggregate public and private investment, the insignificant level of public investment over the period means that the relationship is primarily with private investment (Matale *et al*, 1997:38, 51).

The causality in this relationship is an important issue. The role of private capital flows in increasing the supply of funds for investment — and, in the case of FDI, in increasing investment directly — suggests that increases in capital flows may lead to higher domestic investment. Equally, however, a rise in domestic investment may attract higher capital inflows by signalling an increase in confidence among domestic investors (who are presumed to have superior "insider" access to information on the economy and economic policy) or simply by leading to a rise in imports of capital goods and hence in related external financing. Finally, changes in other factors — such as interest rates and rates of return more generally as well as other aspects of the economic and policy environment — may cause both domestic and foreign investment to change, leading to a positive correlation despite the absence of any causal relationship.

In Zimbabwe, the positive relationship between capital flows and domestic investment combined with the absence of causality suggests that the third explanation advanced above — of common variables influencing both capital flows and domestic investment — may be the most appropriate (Kufeni *et al*, 1997).

In South Africa, however, the causality appears to have run in different directions during different periods. Between 1961 and 1984, peaks and troughs in net capital movements tended to follow, with a lag of up to 12 months, peaks and troughs in domestic fixed investment, suggesting that domestic investment may have been attracting capital inflows. Between 1984 and 1994, however, exogenous political factors (sanctions) led to a period of sustained capital outflows. The outflows were an important contributory factor to a decline in the growth performance of the economy and a collapse in domestic investment from 25% of GDP in 1984 to 15.5% in 1993. Although part of this decline reflected sharp cutbacks in public investment, cutbacks in private, especially manufacturing, investment were equally significant (Khatri *et al*, 1997:3-9).

The generally positive impact of capital inflows on investment, imports and exports suggests that the impact on growth has also been positive — although the long-term effect may be less healthy if, as in Zambia, capital inflows are increasing consumption (Matale *et al*, 1997:50).

The natural experiment afforded by the so-called financial sanctions on South Africa between 1985 and 1994 provides strong evidence of the direct impact of capital flows on growth. The sustained capital outflows during this period led to an unprecedented decline of more than 12% in real GDP per capita. Conversely, the role of capital inflows in funding capital (and intermediate) imports and investment is found by Khatri *et al* (1997:3-12) to have been "an important contributing factor to the high economic growth of the 1960s and 1970s". The outflow of capital in the late 1980s and early 1990s curtailed growth both through direct effects on investment and by forcing the authorities to apply restrictive policy measures.

A similarly strong relationship between capital inflows and growth is identified in Uganda, where the role of external savings in financing investment is again emphasised. In this case, however, a crucial aspect of the impact of capital flows on growth is the specific role of access to coffee prefinance from foreign sources, a factor identified by Kasekende *et al* (1997:33) as "critical to the recovery in the coffee industry in Uganda".

Another mechanism connecting capital inflows and growth is the role of FDI in facilitating the transfer of modern technology and improving managerial and technical skills. Although this factor was cited in most studies, evidence was not available to test its importance.

6.3 Monetary Policy and Financial Markets

The sharp rise in capital inflows — and occasional outflows — in the 1990s has had a profound impact on monetary conditions, monetary policy and financial markets in all the project countries. The rise in capital flows has been associated with concerted programmes of financial liberalisation and macroeconomic stabilisation, which have profoundly changed in the macroeconomic environment. Moreover, as a result of the increase in international capital flows, changes in net foreign assets have become a more important — and, in many cases, dominant — determinant of changes in the money supply. Capital flows influence inflation and the macroeconomy through their effects not only on interest rates, but also on exchange rates. Finally, the increasing volatility of capital flows has had implications for monetary conditions and for financial markets more generally.

The most evident result has been the sea change in real interest rates. As shown in Figures 6.2a-e, real interest rates were persistently negative in the 1980s in all countries. Liberalisation in the early 1990s led to sharp rises and sustained positive real interest rates in virtually all countries. This is particularly evident in the 1993 interest rate rises in Zambia, Zimbabwe

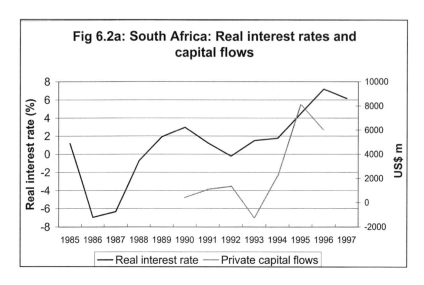

Fig 6.2a: South Africa: Real interest rates and capital flows

and Uganda. The only partial exception to this pattern is Tanzania, which has seen pronounced volatility and a return to negative real interest rates in 1997-8: but this reflects the particular "captive" nature of Tanzania's Treasury Bill market, which reduced the market orientation of the T-Bill rate.

While the shift from negative to positive real interest rates was a necessary and desired outcome of liberalisation and stabilisation, the unexpected persistence of very high real interest rates, in most countries, has raised

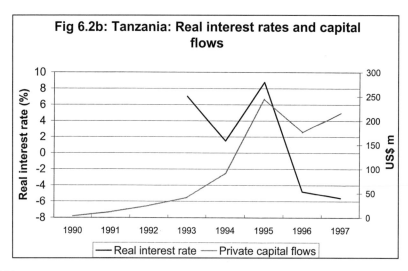

Fig 6.2b: Tanzania: Real interest rates and capital flows

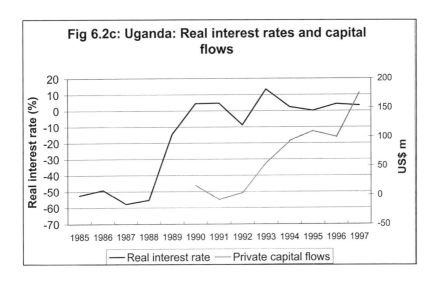

Fig 6.2c: Uganda: Real interest rates and capital flows

questions throughout the region concerning the potential costs associated with the new openness to private capital flows. It is increasingly evident — not least in the aftermath of the Asian Crisis — that the heightened role now played by private capital flows in domestic markets, and the volatility of these flows, is a key factor behind the persistently high real interest rates.

The increase in private capital flows has also affected the volatility of interest rates. The effects of changing capital flows on interest rates depend importantly on the policy stance adopted by the authorities, as discussed further in Chapter 7, as well as on the structure of domestic capital markets. In countries such as Tanzania and Uganda, where concerns about macroeconomic stability have led the authorities more readily to accept an appreciation of the real exchange rate, swings in capital flows have had relatively limited effects on the volatility of domestic interest rates. The link between capital flows and domestic interest rates is strongest in countries, such as South Africa and Zimbabwe, where capital markets are most developed. In Zimbabwe, Kufeni et al (1997:53) find evidence of a strong causal link between capital inflows and interest rates. In South Africa, the discount rate system of monetary policy that was followed until March 1998 meant that short-term interest rates were effectively tied to the "Bank rate" set by the central bank, and hence were unresponsive to capital flows. Long-term interest rates, however, have been highly responsive to international capital movements. The surge in inflows during 1995 led to a large fall in the yields on long-term government stock (Van der Merwe, 1998), and the outflows after the exchange rate crisis in February 1996 raised

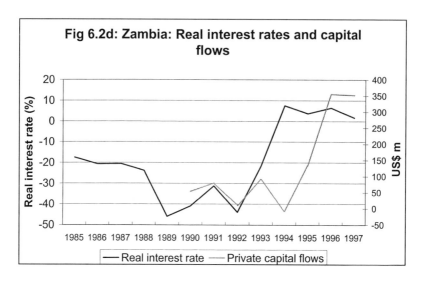

Fig 6.2d: Zambia: Real interest rates and capital flows

yields sharply again.

Another striking recent finding (by Ncube *et al*, 1996) is that international capital movements in South Africa have affected the correlation of domestic interest rates with US interest rates In the first quarter of 1996, for example, when net foreign purchases on the South African bond market were at near record levels, the correlation between domestic bond yields and the yields on US Treasury bonds was 95%. When, however, foreign purchases collapsed in the second quarter, the correlation with US

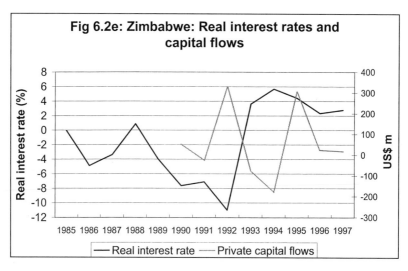

Fig 6.2e: Zimbabwe: Real interest rates and capital flows

interest rates did too — dropping to 4%.

Capital flows also affect monetary conditions through the increased role of net foreign assets in determining changes in the money supply. This is typified by the experience of Uganda, where the increase in net foreign assets has replaced net domestic asset growth as the principal cause of broad money expansion (Kasekende *et al*, 1997:30). In Zimbabwe, too, increases in capital inflows have been associated with increased growth in monetary aggregates, with clear causality from capital flows to aggregates. Money supply growth is, however, more volatile than capital flows, pointing to the continuing importance of domestic factors (Kufeni *et al*, 1997:53).

In South Africa, capital movements have sometimes stabilised the growth in the money supply due to the inverse relationship between the current account balance and net capital flows. Often, however, capital movements have accentuated changes in the rate of increase of monetary aggregates. Since June 1993, when the monetary fluctuations resulting from government financing activities were essentially eliminated by the creation of government "tax and loan" accounts with commercial banks, changes in net foreign assets and in notes and coin in circulation have been the main causes of changes in domestic liquidity. For much of this period, the increased level and volatility of private capital flows has meant that changes in net foreign assets have dominated monetary aggregates (Khatri *et al*, 1997:3-16,18). A striking example of volatility came at the end of 1995, when fluctuating international capital flows resulted in an increase of R5.5 billion of net foreign assets in the fourth quarter of 1995, followed by a decrease of R4.4 billion in the first quarter of 1996 — a swing of 2.2% of GDP.

Capital flows also affect monetary aggregates via changes in domestic credit. This occurs when the flows are the result of domestic producers switching between foreign and domestic sources of finance, typically because of changing interest rates (in domestic and foreign markets) and interest rate expectations. While the depth and liquidity of South African financial markets make this particularly evident in South Africa, it has occurred to varying degrees in all countries.

Finally, capital flows affect monetary conditions, and hence inflationary pressures, via effects on the exchange rate. A rising exchange rate slows the economy, while a depreciating exchange rate will generally stimulate the economy. The rising exchange rates in Tanzania and Uganda during the recent capital inflows helped to offset the potential inflationary pressures of the inflows. In the case of Uganda, the rise has been sufficient, in combination with the tight fiscal stance, to contain inflationary pressures. In Tanzania, private capital flows exerted upward pressure on inflation in

1994-5, suggesting that the dampening effect of the exchange rate appreciation was insufficient.

Overall, there is no doubt that the most important factor behind the recent increased volatility in exchange rates and interest rates in the project countries is the shift to more flexible, market-determined exchange rates and interest rates. Nevertheless, the analysis in the country studies suggests that capital flows have accentuated this volatility. A series of banking sector crises in Tanzania, Uganda and Zambia has resulted from this volatility. Although Africa has, to date, escaped the acute financial instability experienced in Mexico in 1994-5 and in Asia in 1997-8, the narrow, illiquid markets found in most countries are ill-suited to the task of absorbing the large swings in capital flows that have occurred in recent years. The non-existence or narrowness of capital markets, in particular, have made these countries more vulnerable to asset price bubbles and the associated risk of crashes. Even in South Africa, with the deepest and most liquid capital markets in the region, the swings in capital flows experienced since 1994 have dominated the macroeconomic policy environment. It is to these policy challenges that we now turn.

Chapter 7 Policy Responses

Jonathan Leape

While private capital inflows are now being actively encouraged in many African countries, the analysis in the previous chapter suggests that such flows can have negative effects on both the financial and the real sectors of the economy, while the benefits may prove hard to realise.

A key determinant of the balance between these different effects is the policy strategy adopted by government. Where capital flows are large relative to the economy — as in all of the countries studied here — such strategies are crucial to limiting the destabilising effects of capital inflows, and maximising their contribution to growth and investment.

While achieving a variety of macroeconomic or other objectives may represent the primary justification for government intervention, governments increasingly recognise that they have an implicit (or even explicit) liability for servicing private capital flows. The Asian crisis of 1997 shows that this liability constitutes a powerful argument for governments to adopt an active and broad-ranging approach in responding to cross-border private capital flows.

Appropriate policies depend on the availability and flexibility of various instruments, the nature of domestic financial markets, the scale and composition of inflows, the prevailing policy environment and the extent of policymakers' credibility.

In theory, decisions should be guided by the causes and effects of flows. The more they are competitiveness-enhancing and the product of sustainable domestic ("pull") factors, the more justified is an appreciation of the currency. Conversely, the more the inflows are consumption-oriented and the product of short-term, reversible international ("push") factors, the more justified is an accumulation of foreign reserves.

In practice, however, the causes of capital flows are difficult to identify. In this light, other balance of payments and macroeconomic policy objectives predominate and policy is likely to focus on containing vulnerability to possible outflows, and minimising risks of overheating, real exchange rate appreciation, and unsustainable consumption growth.

The key policy options are foreign exchange market intervention, capital account liberalisation, monetary policy and sterilisation, fiscal policy, and financial sector reform and development.

7.1 Foreign Exchange Intervention and Exchange Rate Policy

The most immediate challenge to the authorities has been how to manage the exchange rate and foreign reserves. Faced, for example, by a capital account surplus that outstrips any deficit on the current account, the authorities have to decide whether, or to what extent, to allow an appreciation of the exchange rate or to accumulate foreign exchange reserves so as to limit appreciation.

The two polar policy responses are fixed and floating exchange rates. Under fixed or pegged exchange rates, the central bank is formally committed to acquiring all foreign exchange assets which flow into the economy (in exchange for domestic assets). Under a pure floating exchange rate, the central bank undertakes no foreign exchange intervention and accumulates no reserves. Any surplus on the capital account must therefore be matched by a deficit on the current account, and equilibrium between the two is achieved through an appreciation of the exchange rate.

In the 1980s, many African countries were operating a fixed exchange rate — although typically in a situation of multiple exchange rates as a result of the emergence of parallel markets in foreign exchange. By the mid-1990s, almost all — including all five countries studied here — had unified the foreign exchange market, and shifted to a floating regime. In most countries the shift was gradual, albeit with identifiable milestones. In Tanzania and Zimbabwe, reforms culminated in an official shift from an administered exchange rate to a floating regime (in mid-1993 and early 1994, respectively).

Balance of payments volatility — due, not least, to the increasing volatility of private capital flows — was perceived by the authorities to leave little choice but flexible rates. It is, however, far from clear that countries have reaped the expected benefits. A recent study by economists at the InterAmerican Development Bank suggests that floating exchange rates in the 1990s in some Latin American countries has not enabled an independent monetary policy (Hausmann et al, 1999). Moreover, flexible exchange rates have caused higher real interest rates, smaller financial systems and increased sensitivity of domestic interest rates to changes in international (especially US) rates. These findings echo the experience in Africa. Flexible exchange rates have not yielded greater independence for domestic interest rates: monetary policy remains largely determined by the balance of payments. At the same time, real interest rates have risen, with often severe adverse effects for domestic investment and growth. And in South Africa, where capital markets are most developed, South African interest rates have been increasingly sensitive to international (US) rates (see Chapter 6). Taken together, these effects suggest that the question of the appropriate exchange rate regime for African countries remains open. None of these countries has a "pure" floating exchange rate, opting instead for the common intermediate case of a "managed" float — in which the authorities must decide on the appropriate trade-off between an appreciation of the currency (the default response under a pure float) and an accumulation of foreign reserves (the default response under a fixed regime). An appreciation of the exchange rate may facilitate foreign debt service and keep downward pressure on import prices, but at the cost of undermining competitiveness and growth. On the other hand, an increase in foreign reserves may prevent any fall in competitiveness, but at the cost of unacceptable inflationary pressures (or excessively costly sterilisation, as discussed below). The project countries have followed different strategies in making these trade-offs.

A further complication arises from the fact that traditional exports are priced in US dollars while most non-traditional exports and, especially, most imports are priced in European and regional currencies. This asymmetry implies that any simple measure of the real exchange rate does not fully capture a country's policy objectives (Jenkins and Thomas, 1999).

The scale and volatility of capital flows has led governments to intervene more actively in the foreign exchange market, to manage inflows or to smooth outflows. Deciding on the appropriate exchange rate strategy requires difficult trade-offs. Policymakers in project countries have incomplete information to make these judgements. Nominal appreciation pre-empts inflationary pressure, but excessive appreciation risks undermining the current account and sowing the seeds for future balance of payments crises, hitting non-traditional exporters and import competing industries hardest. On the other hand, intervention to prevent appreciation can provide an important foreign reserves cushion to help offset unexpected outflows, but substantial intervention quickly outstrips the authorities' capacity for sterilisation (see below) leading to destabilising inflation. Given the central role of exchange rate depreciation in adjustment programmes and export promotion, many countries treat appreciation as a serious problem.

In Uganda and Zimbabwe, the central banks have intervened to smooth short-term fluctuations, and to moderate large appreciations (e.g., Kasekende *et al*, 1997:21). In Tanzania, the government has intervened heavily, mostly to prevent depreciation. Yet this has undermined external competitiveness with a 20% real appreciation of the currency in 1994-6 (Kimei *et al*, 1997:38-9).

In Zambia, the exchange rate is a focal point of policy, given high import dependency, and severe external indebtedness. Supply of foreign exchange is vulnerable and unstable as most is derived from copper export receipts and donor aid. Demand, however, is consistently strong and not responsive to policy measures. This means that the exchange rate is the principal mechanism matching supply with demand. Rapidly-growing foreign exchange accounts held by residents have not been exchange rate sensitive in the short-term, because they are mostly importing firms building amounts for imports, and international organisations operating in Zambia (Matale *et al*, 1997:25-6). The authorities also recognise that the exchange rate is important to competitiveness with Zambia's main trading partners but, as shown in Figure 6.1d, they have had mixed success, as the real exchange rate has been volatile and overall has appreciated since 1992.

South Africa's approach differs primarily in the greater scope for intervention afforded by its more developed financial markets. Two features of South Africa's intervention strategy deserve particular attention: the forward market and what might be called "potential" intervention.

By undertaking forward transactions with authorised foreign exchange dealers or by adjusting its own forward rates when the Reserve Bank has itself quoted to the market, the Bank can increase or decrease the supply of dollars to the market (without affecting gross or net foreign reserves). Alternatively, the Bank can undertake foreign exchange swaps — selling forward US dollars to a foreign exchange dealer and buying spot US dollars from the dealer (or vice versa) — to increase or decrease its (spot) foreign exchange reserves. The net effect of a swap transaction is to transfer foreign exchange from the banking sector to the Reserve Bank (or vice versa). For a detailed discussion of these issues see Kahn and Leape (1996) and especially Leape (1998a).

Such swaps are sometimes initiated by the Reserve Bank to fund its intervention in the spot market (by, say, selling US dollars to support the Rand) or to boost its foreign reserves. This is an example of "active" intervention in the forward market. The Reserve Bank also intervenes "passively" in the forward market, when transactions initiated by foreign exchange dealers (reflecting, in turn, forward transactions by private firms and banks) result in a change to the Bank's net forward position. In this case, the decision to allow an increase in forward exposure is a decision to intervene — passively — in the market.

As shown in Box 7.1, South Africa's use of the forward market has dramatically enhanced its ability to intervene in foreign exchange markets, which would otherwise have been severely constrained by the low level of reserves. Forward market intervention has dwarfed spot market intervention. For example, in the rand crisis of 1996, intervention in the forward market exceeded $9 billion, compared to just $1.6 billion from (spot) foreign reserves. This has had undoubted benefits by enabling the Bank to maintain a liquid foreign exchange market — even in times of crisis — and to dampen the volatility of the exchange rate. But, the availability of such a "deep pocket" has also created an incentive for excessive intervention. In addition, the Bank's large resulting forward liabilities have, at times, destabilised the foreign exchange market. These liabilities (the excess of forward sales over forward purchases) have averaged around one-fifth of GDP since 1987, seven times as high as average gross foreign reserves.

Box 7.1 South African Intervention in the Foreign Exchange Market

Intervention in the foreign exchange market in response to capital flows enables authorities to influence the stability of the real exchange rate, liquidity in the foreign exchange market, foreign reserves levels, and inflation. However, attaching a single policy instrument to multiple objectives inevitably leads to conflicts, forcing authorities to make trade-offs.

In the wake of huge capital inflows in 1995 for example, the South African authorities reached the point where further intervention to prevent excessive exchange rate appreciation risked unacceptable inflationary pressure. On the other hand, limiting intervention to moderate its inflationary effects may compromise real exchange rate targets, and efforts to increase foreign reserves. In practice, while intervention in the spot foreign exchange market is straightforward, Leape (1998a) shows that the South African authorities have preferred to intervene to a far greater extent in the forward market (see Figure 7.1). Indeed, over the period 1987 to 1997, changes in the net oversold forward position (total forward sales by the central bank less forward purchases) accounted for 90% of changes in the overall net open position (which reflect intervention on forward and spot markets together).

The significance of forward market intervention is shown clearly also in Table 7.1, which maps the key episodes of capital inflows and outflows since 1994. The first episode saw downward pressure on the Rand as an outcome of political uncertainties in the election period, and the Reserve Bank intervened in the spot and forward markets. In the second episode, strong inflows enabled the authorities to significantly reduce the oversold position on the forward book, and to minimise the adverse effects of excessive accumulation of reserves. In the third episode, shortterm capital flowed out on a large scale, and again the authorities used the forward market well in excess of the spot market while in the fourth, increases in net reserves following a surge in inflows were again more than offset by significantly greater decline in the oversold forward

---

position. The fifth episode was triggered by the collapses in Russia and Indonesia in May 1998, which led to large capital outflows. Thus during periods of capital inflows (Episodes 2 and 4), forward market intervention served to minimise macroeconomic disruption that would have occurred if intervention was limited to accumulation of spot foreign reserves — or if the exchange rate had been allowed to rise sharply. During periods of capital outflows (Episodes 1, 3 and 5), the forward market helped at a time when low foreign exchange reserves limited the scope for intervention in the spot market. Indeed, Table 7.1 shows that, in the most recent two of these outflow episodes, intervention on the forward market has outstripped that on the spot market by a factor of almost five to one.

The Reserve Bank's use of "potential intervention" has also been significant. In early 1995 and again in mid 1997, when reserves were low enough to threaten the credibility of SARB's aims to maintain stable real exchange rate, and liquidity in the foreign exchange market, SARB sent signals to the market that the central bank has access to extensive credit lines from international banks, and hence has greater capacity (potential) to achieve its aims through intervention.

Source: Leape (1998a)

Table 7.1 SARB Intervention in Spot and Forward Markets
(millions of dollars)

	Change in net oversold forward position	Change in net foreign reserves position
Episode 1: Jan 1994 - Apr 1994	-1,050	-1,993
Episode 2: Jan 1995 - Jan 1996	13,259	2,368
Episode 3: Feb 1996 - Oct 1996	-9,209	-1,610
Episode 4: Feb 1997 - Feb 1998	5,155	2,097
Episode 5: May 1998 - Jun 1998	-7,814	-1,884

Source:
Leape (1998a); updated using SARB data.

A second important feature of South Africa's recent strategy has been "potential" intervention. The Reserve Bank has repeatedly complemented intervention in spot and forward markets with signals of its ability and willingness to intervene, if necessary. In particular, it has used international credit lines — that is, potential borrowed reserves — as an instrument for influencing the markets. The role of "potential" reserves in intervention

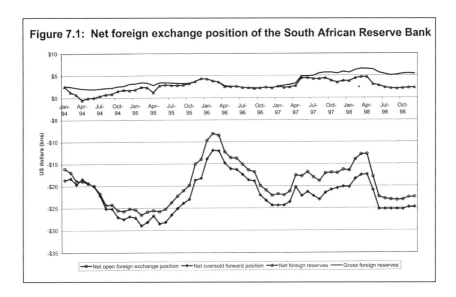

Figure 7.1: Net foreign exchange position of the South African Reserve Bank

Legend: Net open foreign exchange position · Net oversold forward position · Net foreign reserves · Gross foreign reserves

"is created by the fact that the foreign exchange markets... are driven by expectations. Foreign exchange transactions undertaken today will be heavily influenced by agents' expectations of future exchange rates. And just as the various participants in the foreign exchange markets will attempt to identify possible future influences on the exchange rate coming from the current and capital accounts, they will also take account of expected intervention by the central bank" (Leape, 1998a:38).

In this context, the greater a central bank's access to international credit lines, the greater will be its perceived ability to intervene, and the more weight will be given to those aims by agents in the market. In the South African context, persistently low foreign reserves have threatened to undermine the Reserve Bank's credibility in intending to stabilise the real exchange rate and maintain a liquid foreign exchange market. This was particularly true when the government was proposing to liberalise exchange controls — notably the commitment in late 1994 to abolishing the financial rand (dual exchange rate) system. Foreign reserves remained below two months' import cover — less than the three months' the Reserve Bank had set as a precondition for further liberalisation. Therefore the Bank's strategy in early 1995 was to inform the markets that it had arranged substantial international credit lines which, together with existing gross reserves, took the total "potential" reserves well above three months' cover (Leape, 1998a:37-8).

7.2 Capital Account Liberalisation

While the foreign exchange intervention discussed above, and the sterilisation measures discussed below, focus on mitigating the adverse effects (and promoting the positive effects) of capital flows, capital account liberalisation allows countries to work to change the flows. The liberalisation itself, and the way in which it is undertaken, can influence the level, composition and volatility of capital flows. Liberalisation of controls on non-residents is likely to lead to increased inflows — although the short-term effect may be the reverse if there is pent-up demand for foreign exchange (e.g. to repatriate earnings). Liberalisation of controls on residents can provoke excessive foreign inflows through increased outflows by residents, but may also facilitate the return of flight capital. The selective maintenance — or imposition — of controls can alter the nature and level of foreign inflows.

The focus to date in project countries has been on liberalising the capital controls used historically to protect the balance of payments. Increasingly, however, they are considering the potential role of measures such as taxation of inflows and special reserve requirements on foreign credits as valuable instruments for managing the macroeconomic impact of swings in capital flows. All countries are liberalising their capital accounts, but there is active debate on appropriate speed and sequencing and on the final objective. The principal regulatory issue is how best to ensure that mechanisms are in place, when controls are lifted, to limit the systemic risk associated with foreign exchange transactions by resident banks and companies. The Asian crisis illustrated how capital controls have a regulatory function which goes far beyond protecting the balance of payments. The crisis also highlighted the continuing role for government intervention arising from the implicit (and sometimes explicit) government guarantees created by cross-border capital flows.

Liberalisation of controls also requires countries to take steps to protect the tax base. In the corporate sector, countries must introduce "thin capitalisation" and "transfer pricing" regulations to prevent profit shifting, while being careful not to discourage new investment. Such regulations, common in OECD countries, prevent companies from using corporation tax, in particular the tax deductibility of interest payments — to reduce or eliminate their tax payments in host countries. In the personal sector, tax rules for investments made abroad require attention.

The sequencing, timing, speed, consistency and credibility of reforms are critical issues. The regulatory roles implicitly performed by capital controls indicate that early liberalisation of the capital account may have a devastating impact on the financial sector and, to a lesser extent, on the tax base. It is widely agreed therefore that capital account liberalisation should follow the current account and go hand in hand with regulatory reform, and should not be undertaken prematurely in countries with weak domestic financial systems (see, for example, the literature survey in Kasekende and Martin, 1995). Capital account liberalisation is best undertaken gradually, focussing first on FDI and trade-related flows (Fischer and Reisen, 1992). Consistency of macroeconomic, financial and exchange rate policy is vital above all (see, for example, Schadler *et al*, 1993).

One of the most striking findings to emerge from the country studies is the extent to which current account liberalisation led to a *de facto* liberalisation of the capital account. This is most evident in Uganda and Tanzania, where Kasekende *et al* (1997) and Kimei *et al* (1997) find evidence of significant capital inflows coming through the porous current account and, in particular, through foreign exchange bureaux. The same pattern was evident earlier in South Africa, where capital flight via the liberalised current account was substantial (see, for example, Kahn, 1991).

From 1993, countries have been liberalising the capital account, but the timing and sequencing have diverged tremendously. Zambia adopted a "big bang" approach, completely liberalising in 1995. Its decision was driven primarily by a desire to signal government commitment to liberalisation. The government was convinced that controls were preventing private capital inflows, and judged that a gradual approach would lead investors to wait and see whether reforms persisted. Initially, the liberalisation provoked large outflows, including repatriations already in the pipeline: many international bankers used the chance to test government commitment to reform. Only when reforms persisted did inflows begin to resume, highlighting the importance of government credibility as a determinant of the impact of liberalisation measures.

Uganda also announced complete liberalisation in July 1997. By 1998, the reform had provoked interest by foreign fund managers in shilling denominated assets, including EADB bonds and promissory notes, although it was too soon to assess the overall impact (Kasekende *et al*, 1997:24).

Other countries have been more cautious, following a gradual approach. Tanzania's initial response to inflows both official and private was to liberalise the exchange regime (Kimei *et al*, 1997:32-6). However, the government was very cautious in 1995-7 for fear of outflows, and was not convinced that liberalisation would increase inflows.

South Africa, too, has followed a gradual approach. Priority was given to abolishing all restrictions on non-residents, and abolishing the "financial rand" mechanism — a dual exchange rate system that applied to all investments by non-residents — in March 1995. Once controls on non-residents had been eased, priority in liberalising restrictions on residents was given to relaxing controls on outward investment by institutional investors. The case for this sequence was strong. In the first place, pension funds and life insurers hold a dominant portion of personal savings and needed international diversification in their portfolios. Secondly, the reporting mechanisms for institutional investors required for prudential regulatory purposes provided a straightforward means for monitoring outflows. Finally, the large domestic liabilities of these institutions (associated with future pension and insurance payouts) provided a natural limit to their desired foreign investment. For these reasons, relaxing controls on institutional investors was a useful instrument for the phased liberalisation of controls on individuals. By contrast, relaxing direct controls on individuals or companies was recognised to cause monitoring problems — though by 1996 measures were being introduced allowing foreign currency holdings by individuals and easing restrictions on foreign direct investment by firms (Kahn and Leape, 1997).

A distinguishing feature in South Africa has been a concerted — and largely successful — effort to minimise market and macroeconomic disruption. This has had three main components. The first has been to implement reforms gradually. This minimised the impact of the reforms by restricting the volume of funds involved and also enabled the government to adapt the pace and strategy of liberalisation in light of the initial private sector response. The second has been to establish appropriate fiscal and regulatory frameworks before reforms (e.g., by tightening the fiscal position since 1994 and formalising all government guarantee arrangements in 1997). The third has been careful management of private sector expectations in the lead up to changes. The 1995 abolition of the financial rand provides the most striking example. Extensive "leaks" about the imminence of abolition, and about the central bank's assessment of the post-reform value of the currency, closed the gap between primary and secondary exchange rates in the three months before abolition. The government then announced abolition after close of business on Friday and was able to open the newly unified foreign exchange market on Monday with no perceptible disruption to the large volume of foreign exchange transactions on current and capital accounts.

Gradualism has produced internal and external criticism about the slow pace of reform, but it has also helped to prevent policy reversals — even in the face of currency crises in 1996 and 1998.

Zimbabwe has also followed a gradual approach, although with less success. In 1994, corporate and individual foreign currency accounts were allowed. Other liberalisation measures include 100% remittance of profit and dividends, foreign exchange bureaux and the abolition of export surrender requirements (Kufeni *et al*, 1997:56). However, liberalisation has not proved sustainable. In September 1998, the government responded to a depreciation of 50% in the space of a few days by reimposing wide-ranging controls on the capital account and current account. These policy reversals have created considerable uncertainty as to the future of Zimbabwe's liberalisation and raised questions regarding the strength of the political commitment to reform. But they also suggest that the pace and sequencing of the earlier liberalisation programme may have been inappropriate.

When the capital account has been liberalised, will selective reintroduction of capital controls prove useful in managing capital flow surges, or possible capital flight? Outflows are difficult to control, and capital flight will occur under even the tightest control regime. Controls will also be of little benefit if not accompanied by sound domestic macroeconomic management. Helleiner (1996) argues that Sub-Saharan Africa's strategy of allowing the exchange rate to adjust to the level of flows has produced much less satisfactory results than East Asian and Latin American policy mixes of foreign exchange intervention, sterilisation, fiscal discipline, and careful use of direct controls on inward and outward flows to dampen volatile short-term movements.

One instrument widely employed in a range of countries — but not in Africa — is special reserve requirements for foreign borrowing. These are sometimes called "variable deposit requirements" or VDRs. These are imposed as non-interest-bearing reserve requirements — deposits held with the central bank — paid and denominated in foreign currency. VDRs represent an effective tax on foreign credits, which works to discourage inflows. In addition, the requirements have a potentially useful impact on domestic liquidity, both directly and indirectly (Schadler *et al*, 1993; Reinhart and Dunaway, 1995; Lee, 1996; and Leape, 1998a). VDRs are flexible because they can be adjusted by the authorities in a number of ways. The most basic is the percentage. A second is the minimum deposit period (this can influence the maturity structure of foreign credits, as the effective tax associated with any specified deposit holding period will be greater the shorter the maturity of the credit). A third is applying the VDR differentially to new and existing credits, allowing a higher effective tax to be imposed on new borrowings.

These features have made VDRs an attractive instrument for influencing the level and the maturity structure of foreign borrowing by domestic residents, as demonstrated by Spain and Chile. Another significant advantage is their ability to enhance authorities' efforts to manage the impact of capital inflows on domestic liquidity and aggregate demand. By retaining in the central bank a fraction of new foreign credits (through the required deposits), VDRs directly reduce the impact of the inflows on the monetary base, thereby reducing the need for sterilisation. In addition, as non-interest bearing reserve requirements generate revenue for the central bank, VDRs avoid – and, in a minor way help to offset - the potentially high quasi-fiscal costs of other sterilisation measures (such as open market operations), thereby increasing the scope for such measures.

VDRs could prove a useful addition to the set of instruments employed in Sub-Saharan Africa. Since VDRs are a form of capital control (albeit a market-oriented one), it is sensible to maintain the credibility of government commitment to liberalisation by using them sparingly — to minimise the risk that investors perceive essentially prudent controls as policy reversals. Moreover, VDRs must be used by governments as a complement to — not a substitute for — appropriate monetary and fiscal policies.

Relatedly, there has, to date, been little discussion in the project countries of the possibility of using taxation as an instrument to reduce the level or alter the composition of capital inflows, despite the active international debate on the "Tobin tax" and other proposals to tax cross-border capital transactions (see, for example, Obstfeld, 1995). Taxes deserve further attention, as they cause less distortion in foreign exchange and financial markets than direct controls, and have the benefit of raising fiscal revenues. A tax on short-term speculative inflows has attracted increasing attention as an instrument for increasing speculation costs. Drawing on experiences in Latin America and Asia, some have argued forcefully in favour of such measures (Griffith-Jones 1995, Dornbusch 1997, Williamson 1994). Though others have argued that they are temporary measures and likely to prove ineffective (Schadler *et al*, 1993; Mathieson *et al*, 1993), there is now a growing consensus (see, for example, BIS, 1995a and 1995b) that selective capital controls are an essential weapon in the policy armoury, if accompanied by sound macroeconomic management.

Yet practical difficulties currently prevent their implementation in Africa. Inadequate data make it unlikely that governments could consistently distinguish between speculative flows and productive flows. Attempts to impose controls on loans or deposits might lead to evasion by over- and under-invoicing of goods, a private sector return to the parallel financial market, and channelling capital inflows through the subsidiaries of foreign companies (making them direct investment rather than loans or deposits). In addition, the introduction of controls may wrongly be taken as an attempt to reverse policy, and therefore undermine credibility and adjustment.

7.3 Monetary Policy

A third key aspect of the policy response concerns measures to influence domestic prices and aggregate demand. The problems are most acute during large capital inflows. If the authorities try to limit the upward pressure on the exchange rate by accumulating foreign reserves, the central bank's net holdings of foreign assets will rise, leading to an increase in the monetary base. The short-term macroeconomic policy response to capital flows, and management of their impact, begins with monetary policy.

The issue is how to manage the central bank's balance sheet so as to achieve the desired effect on the monetary base, by reducing other components to offset excessive growth in net foreign assets caused by capital inflows. Most important among these other components are net lending to government (the fiscal deficit), and changes in the amount of currency in circulation. If the authorities limit growth in these other components, it may be possible to "sterilise" the impact of capital inflows (and outflows). Recent assessments of sterilisation measures in developing countries include Helleiner (1996), Reinhart and Dunaway (1996) and Reisen (1996).

As recent experience in Africa and elsewhere has highlighted the problems of sudden capital outflows, it is important also to highlight that if these cause a drop in foreign exchange reserves, monetary policy to inject liquidity is essential to preventing an excessive monetary contraction.

The policy instruments employed by the monetary authorities to sterilise the impact on domestic liquidity are the same as those used more generally for liquidity management. They can be divided into "market" and "non-market" operations. The former include all forms of open market operations and other measures such as foreign exchange swaps; the latter include changes in statutory reserve requirements, which have proved especially important in the region, and other instruments such as transfers of government deposits between commercial and central banks. It is also important to bear in mind that, by keeping interest rates high, sterilisation can perpetuate large inflows, and prevent inflows from increasing domestic investment and growth. It can also involve unsustainable quasi-fiscal costs.

The underdeveloped state of securities markets in most African countries severely circumscribes the scope for sterilisation. Unsterilised foreign exchange intervention in the face of capital inflows leads to reserves accumulation and increases the money supply. While this puts downward pressure on interest rates and thus may curtail inflows, without a corresponding increase in money demand it causes inflation, and forces up the real exchange rate. This has often been "the first line of defence" for many African countries in the absence of sterilisation options.

This is certainly true for Uganda, which has had minimal success in

137

containing monetary growth through monetary policy in a liberalised financial system. Liberalising interest rates and issuing government or central bank bills have been undermined by thin and underdeveloped financial markets. The problem has been aggravated by distressed banking systems, the volatility of money demand and multipliers, and elements of reserve money that are beyond the control of the central bank. This raises the need for tight fiscal policy (see below) to supplement sterilisation efforts through the issue of Treasury Bills (Kasekende *et al*, 1997:23).

In Zambia, however, nominal interest rates were raised sharply in response to high inflation in 1994, and successfully limited excessive domestic credit expansion and encouraged higher domestic savings. Open market operations were introduced only in 1995. Matale *et al* (1997) conclude that they have so far been "successful in influencing short-term liquidity in the domestic money market", but future desirability of this policy option in Zambia is reduced by its "large cost particularly in respect to deposits taken".

Tanzania's reliance on monetary policy and interest rates to ease the effects of the 1994-5 coffee price boom was, in the view of Kimei *et al*, "excessive". The centrepiece of the government's sterilisation strategy was a proposal to place medium and long-term government securities with the non-bank sector. The proposal was, however, watered down, and the authorities instead issued floating certificates of deposit to non-bank financial institutions at a negotiated rate of 31%. The slack was partly picked up by other policies, especially heavy use of changes in reserve requirements, as discussed below under "non-market" monetary measures. The government also tightened releases of pipelined debt conversion proceeds and suspended the "Gold Purchase Scheme" of the Bank of Tanzania. In addition, however, the effects of the boom were blunted by the withdrawal of donor assistance in November 1994 following the government's tax evasion scandal (Kimei *et al*, 1997:36-7).

Market-oriented monetary measures in South Africa have taken two forms: open market operations and foreign exchange swaps. Until March 1998, open market operations played an important role in sustaining a money market shortage, which forced commercial banks to make use of the discount window, in turn tying short-term market interest rates to the official Bank rate. Since then, under a new system for monetary policy based on a daily tender via repurchase transactions, open market operations have been used to ensure that banks are always participating in the daily tender, but money market interest rates are now determined by the daily tender, rather than tied to an official rate. Unusually by international standards, open market operations in South Africa historically involved long-term government securities. This was due to a persistent shortage of short-term government paper, which banks required (as collateral) to access the refinancing facilities at the Reserve Bank and to comply with liquid asset requirements.

Another important feature has been the dual role of the Reserve Bank in the market for government securities — as funding agent for the government in both primary and secondary markets, and as principal in using market operations to implement monetary policy. Conflicts between the two roles were inevitable — and emerged in the Bank's use of pre-funding and over-funding in the primary market to reduce liquidity — both of which raised the government's cost of funding. This dual role ended in April 1998, when a set of government-appointed private market-makers took over responsibility for government funding. The shift to a repo system and introduction of private market-makers has increased the role of short-term instruments and the responsiveness of short-term interest rates, thereby enhancing the effectiveness of open market operations as a policy tool for responding quickly to swings in capital flows (Leape, 1998a).

Even more important in liquidity management has been the use of foreign exchange swaps. Particularly where there are autonomous increases in liquidity as a result of increases in net foreign assets, the Reserve Bank has frequently used swaps to manage the money market shortage. More generally, when faced by a shortage of instruments for open market operations, swaps have offered a useful alternative market instrument for reducing liquidity. To drain liquidity from the banking system, foreign exchange held by the Reserve Bank is sold spot to banks against a forward repurchase by the Bank, with the foreign currency then placed on deposit in the banks' names at the Reserve Bank. In this way, the Bank shifts foreign exchange from the Reserve Bank into the banking system in exchange for domestic liquid assets, reducing the monetary base. When faced by capital outflows, the Bank buys spot and sells forward for the purposes of injecting liquidity, which also has the effect of temporarily increasing the level of foreign reserves held by the Reserve Bank. If, in this case, the money market shortage is the result of capital outflows, the Bank's interest in increasing liquidity is likely to coincide with a desire to increase its supply of foreign reserves for intervention purposes. These instruments have had considerable success in offsetting the adverse macroeconomic effects of swings in capital flows. When, for example, South Africa experienced a sharp reversal of capital flows in early 1996 — a swing equivalent to two percent of GDP in the space of a few months — domestic liquidity changed by less than R1bn (Leape, 1998a).

Limits to market-oriented monetary measures. Despite their many advantages, these measures also have costs. Among the most serious are the "quasi-fiscal" costs of sterilisation. Regardless of the form of market intervention, sterilisation ultimately involves the authorities exchanging typically high-yield domestic bonds for low-yield foreign exchange. Where the interest differential is substantial — as it has been in every African country — so is the direct quasi-fiscal cost. Also important is the upward pressure on domestic interest rates created by such measures and the associated opportunity cost in debt service as well as the crowding out effects on private credit. Moreover, the rise in interest rates may stimulate further capital inflows, thus aggravating the problem.

In addition, sterilisation measures based on open market sales of domestic bonds will only reduce liquidity to the extent that investors do not regard them as perfect substitutes for foreign bonds. And with the liberalisation of exchange controls, financial institutions find it increasingly easy to adjust their foreign exchange positions following government intervention so as to maintain their desired portfolio — and thereby to undermine the impact of the monetary intervention.

Finally, even in those countries with more developed financial markets, such as Zimbabwe and South Africa, the central banks have often simply lacked the supply of domestic bonds necessary to carry out sustained open market operations. In some instances, this has led to the issuance of central bank bills for the purposes of open market operations.

7.4 Non-Market Measures

Non-market operations, including transfers of public sector deposits and especially changes in reserve requirements, have also played an important role in liquidity management in response to swings in capital flows.

Transfers of public sector deposits. The shifting of government deposits between private banks and the central bank has proven internationally to be an effective means of sterilisation. Since 1993, the South African government has maintained "Tax and Loan Accounts" (TLAs) with private banks in addition to its Exchequer Account with the Reserve Bank. An important function of the TLAs has been to minimise the distorting impact on liquidity of government financing transactions. They have also, however, provided an additional discretionary instrument whereby the Bank can alter the money market shortage by shifting deposits from the TLAs to the Exchequer Account or vice versa. Recent developments have, however, sharply reduced their scope. They are largely dependent on the availability of government deposits held at banks when a large inflow of capital takes place. Efforts by the government since 1996, to improve its debt and cash management, so as to reduce interest costs, have largely eliminated such "idle" deposits. The use of transfers of government deposits has been considered in Uganda (Kasekende *et al*, 1997) and elsewhere in the region, but no policy decisions have yet been taken.

Changes in reserve requirements. Much more widespread in the region has been the use of changes in reserve requirements. Raising reserve requirements acts as a tax on the banking system and can work to decrease the money multiplier and limit credit to the private sector. It can also be used counter-cyclically, by targeting the source of a boom. In political economy terms, changes in reserve requirements have the advantage of being an implicit or *hidden* tax that arouses less popular opposition than more explicit taxes. Such requirements can also be used to limit particular types of capital inflow, as discussed above.

Changes in reserve requirements have some limitations. Non-interest bearing reserve requirements act as a tax on bank intermediation, and may widen the spread between lending and deposit rates and stimulate disintermediation, as borrowers shift to (un-taxed) non-bank financial institutions. This will undermine monetary control, weaken regulation and supervision and damage the efficiency of the financial system by pushing borrowers towards less efficient lenders. Moreover, the active use of changes in the cash reserve requirement to manage liquidity changes will interfere with banks' portfolio management strategies.

Changes in reserve requirements have, nevertheless, often been used in the region. Tanzania has relied heavily on them since 1987. From 1993, the cash reserve requirement was raised eight times, reaching its highest levels to combat the effects of the 1994-5 coffee boom. The minimum reserve requirement was raised from 8 % in June 1994 to a peak of 18% in June 1995 and was only lowered to 12% in March 1996 (Kimei *et al*, 1997:36, 38).

Zimbabwe has also used changes in reserve requirements to manage destabilising capital flows. Most recently in September 1998, when balance of payments pressures led to a collapse of the exchange rate, the policy measures adopted included a rise in the reserve requirements from 20 to 25% for commercial and merchant banks and from 4 to 5% for finance houses.

Even after shifting to a market-oriented approach to monetary policy, South Africa has occasionally used changes in reserve requirements to support market operations, especially in response to large and sudden changes in domestic liquidity. When surging capital inflows exhausted the scope for market instruments in early 1995, the Bank raised the minimum reserve requirement of banks from 1 to 2% of their total liabilities to the public.

141

In contrast to the foregoing examples, Uganda has avoided increasing reserve requirements. The principal reason has been a recognition that weaknesses in the financial sector made it impossible to implement such requirements effectively. If anything, requirements have been substantially reduced on certain deposits in support of financial sector development objectives.

The potential costs of reserve requirements — to monetary control, effectiveness of regulation and financial sector development — indicate that countries must avoid excessively high levels, but experience in the region shows they can be useful against large sustained changes in liquidity. A key issue looking forward is how to fine tune such requirements to target them more effectively. One example is targeting reserve requirements to specific types of liabilities (for example to off-shore borrowing of banks) as discussed above. A second is the use of supplementary cash requirements against increases in the banks' liabilities from a certain date, rather than against the total liabilities, to concentrate the desired impact on current borrowing and lending decisions while reducing overall distortions.

Finally, the sharp increases in the level and volatility of cross-border capital flows have also had implications for monetary policy frameworks throughout the region. The first and most direct effect, as highlighted earlier, is that changes in net foreign assets have become a more important — in many cases, dominant — determinant of monetary conditions. This has forced countries to broaden the range of intermediate targets used in monetary policy. Within that range, the exchange rate has come to play a greater role as an indicator of economic and monetary conditions. In South Africa, for example, the increased magnitude and volatility of capital flows has led to a significant downgrading of money supply targets. Tanzania, Uganda and Zimbabwe have been similarly affected, and have also rethought their money supply targets.

7.5 Fiscal Policy

Fiscal adjustment is also an important part of the policy response to capital flows. By reducing the fiscal deficit, the authorities can mitigate the adverse macroeconomic impact of capital inflows by decreasing the government's own contribution to domestic liquidity. In this way, fiscal adjustment can work to offset potentially inflationary increases in liquidity.

Limits to the scope for monetary operations — in the face of sustained surges of inflows — have placed great pressure on fiscal policy in the project countries. Fiscal restraint has become the primary method to prevent overheating and a real exchange rate appreciation. Some see this as the only long-term policy (Corbo *et al*, 1994; Schadler *et al*, 1993). They suggest expenditure cuts as opposed to tax rises, in order to limit the demand for non-traded goods, but not tradeables (Calvo, Leiderman and Reinhart, 1993). This makes sense because credit availability from huge capital inflows would counteract the effectiveness of the revenue approach, and also because countries have no easy revenue raising solutions, especially where the formal sector is heavily taxed and the informal sector is large. However, reducing government expenditure can have extremely undesirable social consequences and is often a political minefield. The social and political implications of expenditure cuts severely limit their usefulness as a policy response.

Fiscal measures can also influence the level of capital flows. Reductions in deficit financing can put downward pressure on interest rates, which reduces the attractiveness of domestic bonds to foreign investors — and helps to stem inflows. Fiscal adjustment may, through a different mechanism, also prove important in responding to capital *outflows*. When outflows are, at least in part, the product of foreign (or domestic) investor perceptions of macroeconomic weakness or instability, fiscal adjustment is likely to be central to restoring macroeconomic balance and to signalling the credibility of the government's commitment. This type of fiscal adjustment has been central to recent experience in the project countries. Reducing the deficit has been a priority for all in the 1990s, and most have achieved a significant degree of success. While this has usually been primarily driven by structural adjustment (home grown or otherwise), concerns about capital flows and about the impact of the Asian crisis have also been a factor.

The lack of flexible and effective monetary policy instruments in Uganda meant that sterilisation without the support of fiscal policy could have only limited effectiveness. As a consequence, priority was given in the early 1990s to budgetary control, and significant progress has been made since 1992 in controlling expenditure and boosting revenue mobilisation. Government has become a substantial net lender to the banking system. The budget has been managed flexibly, using cashflow budgeting in coordination with the monetary authorities. This is achieved by cutting or deferring spending to generate savings necessary for orderly absorption of capital inflows and to keep inflation in check. However, beyond a certain level, Uganda has experienced difficulties in generating sufficient savings. The authorities are constrained by the fact that "expenditure is already at critically low levels, and the potential to increase revenue is limited" (Kasekende *et al*, 1997:22).

Tanzania has also taken steps to bring spending under more effective control — as discussed further below — and to enhance revenues. Interestingly, efforts to boost revenues led in 1997 to the decision to end the (mainly fiscal) incentives provided under the National Investment Promotion and Protection Act (1990). These included tax exemption on specified capital and intermediate imports by foreign investors, and the five-year tax holiday (Kimei *et al*, 1997:41).

Zimbabwe has had less success. Political problems have hampered the development of effective mechanisms for expenditure control, with the result that fiscal deficits have stayed stubbornly high — in contrast to the downward trend in most of the region. One aspect of fiscal policy where Zimbabwe has set an example for the region, however, is in boosting revenues by fighting tax evasion. 'Operation Tax Net' and 'Operation Bhadharai' (meaning Operation Pay) in 1997 netted huge additional revenues through spot visits and closer examination of goods (Leape, 1999). These high-profile enforcement exercises have the additional benefit of raising revenues through increased voluntary compliance.

While these short-term measures as well as the continuing attempts to contain fiscal deficits have all been important, several countries have gone further and implemented changes in institutional frameworks, in order to enhance credibility by increasing the clarity of the governments' medium and long-term fiscal policy programme, and by raising the cost of policy reversals — announcing the abandonment of a new institutional framework would be far more costly for policymakers than simply failing to achieve some *ad hoc* fiscal target (Leape, 1999). One example was Zambia's decision in 1993 to adopt a cash budget, to end a spiralling fiscal deficit and macroeconomic instability by requiring that authorisation of spending match the accrual of revenues. A cash budget provides a formal institutional framework which sharply decreases discretionary powers in the authorisation of spending. The government's public commitment to the framework or 'rule' makes it costly for officials or politicians to violate the rule. The cash budget thus operates as a credible public constraint on spending. The impact of the cash budget in Tanzania has been dramatic. Kimei *et al* (1997:44) argue that "whereas fiscal improvement in 1991/92 was brought about by tightening expenditure under the first year of the ESAF1, the 1995/96 outturn was the result of adoption of a cash-based budget".

A second example is the recent adoption by South Africa of a medium–term expenditure framework (MTEF). The MTEF was announced by the Minister of Finance in December 1997 and was implemented in the 1998 Budget. As with the cash budget, the MTEF operates as a public constraint on spending and was adopted largely as a mechanism to enhance the credibility of the government's commitment to fiscal discipline. Its focus, however, is on medium-term spending priorities, rather than the short-run fiscal position.

Enhancing revenues can play as important a role as controlling expenditure, and a number of countries have adopted new institutional frameworks in this context, too. Bureaucratic inertia compounded, in recent years, by increasing pressure on civil service salary bills has, in most African countries, undermined the effectiveness of revenue collection. To the extent that civil service cuts cause a deterioration in enforcement or a growth in corruption, the net effect may, ironically, be a worsening of the fiscal position. Moreover, all too often cuts in salaries and staffing levels create a seedbed for corruption, further weakening enforcement and undermining taxpayer incentives to comply. While a variety of measures have been employed to strengthen tax enforcement — including increases in the budget for enforcement as well as managerial and technical training for revenue personnel — four of the five project countries have also changed the institutional structure of the revenue authorities. South Africa, Tanzania, Uganda and Zambia have granted revenue authorities a substantial degree of autonomy, and established a clear set of objectives and incentives. In all cases the result has been a significant initial increase in revenues collected. However, in Tanzania, Uganda and Zambia, collections have subsequently stagnated, indicating that there are no easy institutional solutions to revenue collection.

7.6 Financial Sector Development

Latin American and South East Asian experiences with capital inflows and reversals show the crucial importance of effective banking regulation and supervision. Surges of capital inflows increase the level of non-performing assets, as cheap finance is made available to less creditworthy borrowers and loans are increasingly made on the collateral of inflated asset prices. This makes the financial sector vulnerable to flow reversals, and therefore to financial crisis. Reducing such vulnerability therefore requires risk management policies including risk-based capital requirements, limits on the foreign exchange exposure of banks, adequate supervision, and the development of effective internal risk management in private banks.

For smaller, and especially developing, economies, "importing" risk management skills and even regulation is likely to be one component of any successful strategy. Carefully reducing barriers to entry for foreign financial institutions may help to reduce the vulnerability of the financial sector. In theory, the entry of international banks can enhance private risk management, by importing risk management systems and improving the quality of credit analysis. In addition, where the international banks come from major financial centres, and continue to be subject to regulation in their home country, the developing market benefits from this more developed regulatory and supervisory framework and there is scope for fruitful cooperation between the two regulatory authorities. Finally, the increased competition may, over time, improve the quality of loans as the pressure on profit margins leads to increased emphasis on credit analysis and sound lending decisions.

Experience in the project countries, however, indicates that these benefits are not alway realised in practice. As discussed in Chapter 4, competition among banks has not improved significantly during the 1990s, in spite of liberalisation of entry barriers. In some cases — notably BCCI and Meridien — the collapse of foreign banks, partly due to the inadequacy of international regulation and supervision, has temporarily undermined the credibility of the whole banking system. In others, the capture of virtually all profitable niche markets by the foreign banks has undermined the indigenous banking sector, contributing to banking collapses. Entry of foreign banks has therefore been no panacea for financial sector development.

These issues have been addressed directly in Uganda in recent years. The 1993 Financial Institution Act empowers the central bank to supervise the banking sector. Prudential requirements were revised in line with Basle standards. Entry and exit barriers have been lifted to encourage competition, and minimum capital requirements of new and existing banks have been increased to better protect depositors. Fortunately, however, Uganda was cautious in letting in new foreign banks, avoiding for example BCCI and Meridien. A deposit insurance fund has been set up, and the open foreign exchange positions of banks have been capped at 25% of core capital. The performance of problem banks has been improved, and the open-ended lending to commercial banks by the central bank, a source of inflationary pressure, has been stopped. However, the financial system remains weak with a high amount of non-performing assets. The Non-Performing Assets Recovery Trust has been set up to recover the bad debts of the Uganda Commercial Bank, but this will require strict supervision. Our country study pointed out the need to address weaknesses in reporting requirements — which was amply borne out by the recent banking sector crisis in Uganda (Kasekende et al, 1997:25).

Zimbabwe, too, has focussed on enhancing its banking supervision, and its amended Banking Act is awaiting ratification by Parliament (Kufeni et al, 1997:56-7). In Tanzania, the Capital Markets and Securities Act (1994) established a legal framework for the development of Tanzania's capital and securities market. The Capital Markets and Securities Authority

(CMSA) was created, with responsibility for overseeing regulations for licensing and supervision of market agents, including dealers and brokers, and provides training and public education (Kimei *et al*, 1997:39).

South Africa benefits from a well-established system of banking regulation and supervision controlled by the Registrar of Banks, based in the central bank. From the mid-1990s, the Registrar was exhorting the major private banks to enhance their internal risk management and advancing the idea of a partnership between them and the central bank. By 1998, the key issue was the overall institutional structure for regulation. Influenced particularly by recent developments in Australia and the UK (where the new Labour government immediately announced that all financial supervision would be integrated into a single regulatory agency, the Financial Services Authority) the government proceeded with a review of the regulatory framework which was expected to reach a conclusion during 1999.

Capital flows have also accelerated other components of financial sector development. The most notable has been pressure to develop, or further develop, capital markets as a vehicle for the efficient allocation of inflowing capital. Many of the countries in the region have given high priority to establishing the legal and institutional framework for capital markets. In Zambia, a stock exchange was established in 1992 and in Tanzania, as discussed above, the framework for capital markets was set out in 1994 and the Dar es Salaam Stock Exchange was established.

In countries where such markets already exist, there has been pressure to develop these markets further. In South Africa, for example, the increasing presence of foreign investors in domestic capital markets has been an important triggering factor behind a series of reforms of the stock and bond exchanges. These include, at the stock exchange, the adoption in March 1996 of automated (screen-based) trading through the Johannesburg Equity Trading (JET) system, fully negotiated fees and dual capacity for brokers. On the bond market, electronic settlement was introduced in 1995 and the process of immobilising scrip in a central depository was launched, listing requirements were tightened and, in late 1997, the exchange shifted to three-day rolling settlement, in line with international best practice (Ncube *et al*, 1996).

Part 4

Conclusions and Recommendations

Chapter 8 Conclusions and Policy Lessons

Jonathan Leape and Matthew Martin

This book has shown that private capital flows to Sub-Saharan Africa have increased dramatically in the 1990s and are highly significant economically. They are also tending towards what are regarded as "less stable" components — portfolio flows and short-term bank loans. In 1997-99, developing countries in all continents have suffered from the volatility of these flows — with frequently catastrophic effects on their growth and development. So what needs to be done to raise the stability and development impact of private capital flows to Africa? And how can African governments protect their economies from the volatility of these flows?

8.1 Monitoring the Flows

A fundamental step for many African countries and international institutions is to improve their monitoring of private capital flows. In most African countries, liberalisation of flows has been unnecessarily accompanied by elimination of monitoring, in contrast to the more prudent practice of other developed and developing economies.

Reversing liberalisation of monitoring is not easy. It will be impossible without sustained efforts to create a "culture of reporting" in the vast majority of countries where this does not exist. Governments have found that they need to educate the public on why it is in their interest to report on flows (so that they can better understand their competitors and create a more open and stable market, and so that government can formulate policies to encourage flows) and on why they should trust government agencies (because they supply reliable information on markets, do not share information with exchange control, investment approval or revenue collection agencies, and implement credible policies to stabilise flows).

Institution-building in government agencies will be essential to effective monitoring. One important aspect is transparent legisation empowering single or multiple agencies to collect data — while restricting their use and dissemination of such data where appropriate. Consultation with the private sector at all stages of collection is equally vital. Any reporting methods must be supported by incentives and penalties to encourage compliance, designed to avoid unnecessary distortions which scare private investors into the parallel market. Investors also want their identities protected, by avoiding asking for details such as customer names or passport numbers, and aggregating flows on a weekly or monthly basis.

However, consultation and surveys need to be selective and targeted, partly to allow greater interaction with respondents, but above all to reduce costs. Countries have found it most effective to reduce data collected to those sources and types of transaction which are essential to policy formulation — or to analysis by market players of the state of the market. They have also been wisest to focus on major transactions, and review and simplify reporting requirements regularly.

Many governments may initially require donor support to cover high recurrent costs of surveys (for postage, stationery, telephone, fax; fuel and transportation to deliver and collect surveys; PC hardware and software; and extra staff time). Agencies normally begin by shortlisting and costing such requirements, and identifying potential internal and donor resources.

Coordination is also vital. African countries can ill afford the inefficiencies associated with duplication of work and poor information flows among different agencies, or with agencies trying to collect information from respondents with whom they have no regular contact. Successful experiences have been where all agencies play a full role in collecting information from their direct "client base" (central banks from banks and bureaux, investment authorities from direct investors, and stock and bond exchanges or capital markets authorities from portfolio investors). Then they need to cooperate to centralise information for balance of payments data aggregation and coordinated policy analysis: to this end, many countries have created inter-departmental balance of payments statistics committees which report policy conclusions to finance ministries, central banks and statistical offices.

Government institutions have also found it necessary to coordinate other bodies. In their absence, academics, international institutions, donors and private sector bodies have been deluging suppliers of capital flows with surveys, resulting in "survey fatigue" and low compliance. Governments may want to sub-contract surveys to such organisations if mutual relations are good and NGOs have comparative advantage, but their data collection for balance of payments and policy formulation is the top priority. Donors and international organisations have a key role in coordination, because they usually fund the surveys by non-government and government agencies: they need to consider developing country national interest and encourage comparative advantage, coordination and information exchange.

Once data are recorded, they are best aggregated in user-friendly computer systems. Many countries need to upgrade recording systems, harmonise those used by different agencies, and create electronic links between primary data sources (stock exchanges, financial institutions and investment authorities) and the central bank and/or finance ministry. This will involve pushing international organisations (Commonwealth Secretariat and UNCTAD) to accelerate their efforts to improve their recording systems to include private sector debt, and to advocate donor funding to upgrade the systems.

Regionally, African countries have much scope for providing bilateral technical assistance to one another — this project has demonstrated that almost every country has an area of expertise which would be useful to others, if donors can be more prepared to fund intra-regional assistance. Coordinated regional targets to reach international data standards might provide an external anchor for individual government policies, but would be ineffectual unless such regional bodies as (in alphabetical order) BCEAO, BEAC, CMA, COMESA, EAC, MEFMI, SACU and SADC (FISCU) give higher priority to recording private capital, and sponsoring training and intra-regional assistance. MEFMI's initiatives to record private debt are most welcome.

African governments are already seeking to match international and regional best practices in monitoring. These involve comprehensive surveys, perhaps beginning with pilot surveys and censuses of stocks and flows. Countries with more advanced monitoring are reassessing the design of their survey forms, frequency, size, and dissemination and processing techniques. On each type of flow, less advanced countries can benefit from their neighbours' advice (for example, on portfolio equity investment, from Kenya, Mauritius, South Africa or Zimbabwe).

Ultimately, countries may want to attain the IMF's internationally recognised standards of data coverage, frequency and timeliness, as a signal to investors of government commitment to improve data and to transparent policy decisions — either the General Data Dissemination System (GDDS) or the more advanced Special Data Dissemination Standard (SDDS). But there is no point in publicly committing to these standards if resource constraints will lead to delay, reversal or lack of government credibility.

8.2 Attracting FDI

The findings of this study indicate that lack of information is one of the most powerful discouragements to investors. Yet when African governments are disseminating information, the increasing diversification of investors by sector and source country highlights the necessity to conduct constant analysis of investor motivations, and to target their investment promotion efforts on sectors and source countries which are the most responsive and motivated. As of 1997, such a targeted policy would have focussed particularly on Asian countries (notably Malaysia, Indonesia and Taiwan), on South African investors elsewhere in the region, and on the activities of the many diverse sub-communities within the "Asian community" in Eastern and Southern Africa (for example targeting Asians living overseas, and those who have already returned and might wish to diversify their businesses when reinvesting earnings). Uganda's example shows that legal and transparent processes for returning seized assets, and targeted publicity campaigns, can achieve far more than blanket investment promotion drives. As for sectors, countries can draw up cost-benefit analyses (from an investor and host nation point of view) of different sectors, similar to those advocated by UNCTAD and, through surveys, target the most dynamic potential sectors.

Similarly, given the rapid changes in their political and economic systems, countries seeking stable FDI flows need to tailor their investment promotion efforts to solving the problems perceived as crucial by investors — which may change dramatically over time.

The *structural barriers* facing investors in Africa are well known. Governments can follow the example of the most dynamic investors in seeking to overcome them, by targeting investment in low cost goods for local markets, or in goods for export to regional neighbours. They can also encourage closer regional cooperation on infrastructure and labour skills so as to ensure that regional trade liberalisation benefits all countries more equitably. Even more interesting is our finding that potential investors still look to governments (rather than the private sector or donors) to supply and regulate the necessary physical and communications infrastructure, to help create and regulate a stable financial infrastructure, and to invest in training and education to improve skills and productivity so that companies can promote Africans to senior managerial or engineering posts. Above all on the training front, governments need to seek ways of encouraging smaller investors to provide their own training programmes, following the example of many successful multinationals, and to set time-bound plans for transferring skilled responsibilities to nationals.

Investors also highly value stable and positive *economic performance.*

154

Governments need to consult the private sector in a transparent and comprehensive manner wherever possible, and to avoid major policy reversals which undermine policy credibility and commitment. In general, particularly given the risks of exogenous shocks, this also implies gradual reforms, particularly in lifting foreign exchange restrictions, to ensure that policies are sustainable; and adjustment programmes which are sufficiently flexible to guard against shocks.

They are also aware that one of their biggest risks is still foreign exchange shortage — another reason why most suggest that the international community should emphasise the stability of aid flows and commodity prices, and provide maximum early debt relief to reduce the liquidity burden of debt service, to underpin a gradual process of external liberalisation. However, many are now equally concerned about the risk of overtaxation or underspending on infrastructure, due to the fiscal burden of debt and the instability of aid flows to the budget, and see greater fiscal debt relief or more stable aid as a means to ensure greater transparency and equity in taxation, in turn encouraging greater tax compliance.

Investors are also realistic about privatisation. It is an important spur to FDI, especially if it can begin with highly profitable industries such as tobacco or breweries rather than with large and politically controversial utilities. They stress measures to accelerate the process between deciding to sell and actual sale, and to make the sales more transparent. But its benefits will be short-lived unless it is reinforced by many other measures to encourage investors.

Another important conclusion is the potential to enhance the role of *investment promotion centres*. Most countries in our study have already made them into proactive one-stop centres, so that they not only travel to sell countries to potential investors, but hand-hold investors through bureaucratic requirements. They have also eliminated duplication of bureaucracy or mandates with sectoral ministries. Yet most centres still lack the resources to track investors after their investment has been approved, so as to continue to assist them in ensuring their investment is pursued successfully. Without a mandate and capacity-building support for such functions, and for the research analysis to support them, both of which are normal in developed country investment promotion centres, a large number of investments will continue not to materialise after they have been approved.

The final set of important factors are political and social. Political stability and strong leadership, and well-publicised measures against crime, corruption and fraud (notably to combat unemployment, to improve the work incentives for civil servants, and increase auditing and fraud inspections) are essential areas for action.

8.3 Stabilising Portfolio Flows

8.3.1 Portfolio Equity Flows

This study has demonstrated once again that portfolio flows are generally the most volatile private capital flows. Stabilising those already present is therefore as important as attracting additional flows. Many elements of such policy are the same as those for FDI (political and economic stability, privatisation, clarification of property rights, and reducing corruption). Even within these broad areas, however, portfolio investors have different concerns such as the "fundamental balance" (current account deficit minus net FDI flows); the tightness of monetary policy which can reduce market liquidity; and a sound banking system.

In seeking to attract portfolio flows, most governments have focussed on promoting the basic structures — notably stock exchanges. National or regional exchanges are important, but not every African country needs its own exchange. If companies in countries without exchanges can list on larger regional exchanges which appear in IFC or Financial Times indexes, they are more likely to attract international investors.

For smaller and national stock exchanges, it is vital to improve procedures, especially on regulation, settlement and custody; to reduce transaction costs; to increase the number of (especially local) companies listed, by creating secondary or over-the-counter markets and selling a small percentage of shares in state-owned companies not targeted for privatisation; to improve information on company performance by tightening accounting and auditing standards, and promoting local brokers, if necessary with capacity-building programmes.

As African governments take such measures, it is to be hoped that IFC and commercial analysts will include more countries in their indices, which can also be a powerful positive influence on investment.

One area of underexploited potential lies in investment funds, particularly those which are already targeting Sub-Saharan Africa, those which are supported by donor institutions with a longer-term perspective and a capacity-building element, and those which are closed-end or attract non-Anglo-Saxon or institutional investors whose flows will be more stable. The managers of these funds have a greater interest than retail investors in maintaining their investment in Africa in times of crisis. However, they have had trouble reaching all but the largest companies.

Nevertheless, even if they are taking all these measures, African governments cannot be assured of stable flows. Global cyclical factors, contagion from other emerging markets and negative perceptions of Africa will continue to make portfolio investors fickle.

8.3.2 *Portfolio Non-Equity Flows*

Another important finding of this study has been the sharply increasing role of non-equity portfolio flows. Most African countries still have few prospects of launching bonds, because they are not perceived as creditworthy and do not have a credit rating, and therefore the cost of any bond would be prohibitive.

For those countries that can issue bonds, their success will depend, above all, on continued macroeconomic stability and credibility of their economic policy framework. This will feed into positive foreign investor perceptions of country credit risk (influenced partly in turn by credit ratings as discussed in Chapter 5). But their success will also be influenced by foreign investors' changing appetites for emerging market risks — a factor almost wholly outside the control of individual governments.

Institutional questions of market structure must also be addressed. Success in attracting foreign investment in domestic securities will rest, in part, on continued efforts to establish a clear legal framework for securities trading, to update information and trading systems and to strengthen administrative procedures for settlement.

The priority for other governments is to monitor and analyse more closely the large and fascinating market in investment in *short-term* Treasury Bills from foreign exchange sources, to identify those which are "foreign" and those which come from resident foreign currency accounts, their relative motivations and impact on monetary policy, and the prospects for issuing longer-term Treasury Bills or domestic bonds in order to reduce liquidity risk, or for discouraging such short-term purchases via taxation or quantitative limits.

8.4 Reviving and Stabilising Bank Lending

Another trend noticed earlier in Africa than in the international data has been the revival of short-term bank lending to the private sector. However, it remains highly volatile and pro-cyclical, so the key challenge is to stabilise such flows.

Meanwhile, long-term lending is still awaiting revival, which will not come until not just commercial debt but overall external debt has been reduced much more dramatically than even under the current HIPC Initiative, freeing countries from both the overhang and liquidity burdens. In contrast, the scope for and benefits of debt-equity conversions are likely to be very limited in highly indebted countries — though they may play a larger role in middle-income or less-indebted countries.

Our most interesting finding on bank lending has been the crucial role of the structure of the banking sector. Multinational banks are essential to the financing of larger multinational companies and major projects, and bring vital access to international correspondent banks. Fortunately, they appear to be reversing somewhat their earlier withdrawal from Africa, but they still need convincing to broaden their client base to local and smaller companies.

The other strong conclusion is the central role of financial sector liberalisation and reform. There are many ways in which the current design of reform (or the partial stage reached) is discouraging bank lending. Liberalisation of foreign exchange regulations is providing a pool of foreign currency funds to replace externally sourced bank lending for small businesses. High yield government domestic debt is allowing banks to avoid needing to lend to make profits, while government arrears reduce assessments of private sector creditworthiness for lending. Oligopolistic banking systems lead to huge profits from local currency lending (or huge losses which prevent any lending) and poor information flows and support services for investors. There are no easy answers in a long struggle to create a healthy banking system and above all to diversify types of institutions.

But governments and donors can take some more immediate steps: by reducing risk through cofinancing and guarantees of private bank loans; by organising regular direct information flows to OECD central banks and encouraging them to be more flexible in provisioning guidelines; and by encouraging OECD export credit agencies to expand their cover for medium-term lending to the private sector, where this is compatible with debt sustainablility.

8.5 Improving Credit Ratings

Insofar as credit ratings influence international capital market perceptions of Africa, our research makes a powerful case for improving their country coverage, methodology and treatment of Sub-Saharan Africa.

As only South Africa in our sample is rated by formal agencies — and the other countries should not want to be until they are more creditworthy — the focus needs to be on the informal agencies.

Country coverage needs extending to all SSA countries with reliable economic data. The methodology of credit agencies could be improved by providing more accurate data, giving priority to (i) providing a clear explanation of their methodology; (ii) moving away from subjective surveys — or at least improving the quality of information supplied to and the diversity of the survey sample; (iii) reducing scope for subjective interpretations and projections by analysts based on out-of-date or short-term economic data trends; and (iv) concentrating on objective measurement of risk disaggregated by different types of capital flows, and backed by detailed well-informed analysis. One example of good practice in this area is the recent methodological improvements undertaken by the Economist Intelligence Unit in their country surveys.

8.6 Macroeconomic Impact

Private capital flows have had pervasive effects on African economies in the 1990s. While all the countries examined in this study benefited from the surge in private capital flows to developing countries in this period, internal developments — notably, the acceleration of financial sector reform and the liberalisation of exchange controls — have been the most important determinants of the timing of flows and of their macroeconomic impact.

By freeing key prices — most importantly the exchange rate and interest rates — the reforms have created a set of transmission mechanisms via which changes in cross-border capital flows have important real and monetary effects on the economies. The magnitude of the swings in key macroeconomic variables reveals the importance of the continuing rigidities in these economies — arising from factors such as incomplete markets, underdeveloped sectors, and high information and transaction costs. This, in turn, highlights the costs of inappropriate sequencing of reforms — and, in particular, of allowing financial liberalisation to proceed rapidly while structural reforms to the real economy lag behind.

The macroeconomic effects of swings in private capital flows are evident in the balance of payments; in savings, investment and growth; and in the level of real interest rates, monetary conditions and financial market volatility.

Balance of payments. Throughout Africa, the balance of payments has long been driven by swings in commodity prices, and other developments affecting the current account. Exports are dominated by primary goods, and all too often by a single crop or metal (coffee in Tanzania and Uganda or copper in Zambia). In the 1990s, however, the sharp rise in private capital flows has become an important determinant of the balance of payments.

Through the 1980s, dependence on primary exports combined, in most cases, with a large external debt, contributed to persistent overvaluation of the (official) exchange rate — a problem that was exacerbated by fixed exchange rate policies. The result was the emergence of parallel foreign exchange markets and, typically, a multiplicity of exchange rates. In this environment, it was difficult if not impossible to identify exchange rate effects of changes in the balance of payments.

The liberalisation of foreign exchange markets led to the elimination of parallel markets in the first half of the 1990s. While unification of the foreign exchange market has resulted in exchange rates that are significantly more volatile than the previous "official" exchange rates, part of the increase has simply reflected the volatility that was earlier confined to the parallel markets. Part of the increase in volatility, however, stems from the sharply higher volumes and volatility of private capital flows being experienced in all countries in this study.

Private capital inflows have, in all countries, been associated with an appreciation of the real exchange rate — and capital outflows have quickly led to falls in the exchange rate. In many countries, such as Tanzania, Uganda and Zambia, underdeveloped financial markets have severely circumscribed the scope for sterilisation of capital flows and the overriding importance of maintaining macroeconomic stability has led to heavy reliance on the exchange rate as an adjustment mechanism. Even in countries with more developed money and capital markets, such as South Africa and Zimbabwe, the broader set of monetary policy instruments has proved insufficient to prevent appreciation in periods of heavy inflows (and depreciation in the face of outflows).

Savings, investment and growth. An important aspect of the overall macroeconomic impact of capital flows in these countries is the effect of such flows on the level of investment and savings. While the evidence available from the project countries suggests some tentative findings with respect to investment and growth, relatively little can be said about the effects on savings. This is, in part, the result of weaknesses in the economic analysis of savings, but it is also a product of the weakness of available data where savings statistics in national accounts data are typically residuals.

Perhaps the most important difficulty in identifying the impact of capital flows on domestic savings is that any possible effects are almost certainly swamped by the effects of inflation (where extremely high levels in some countries have depressed savings); of weaknesses in financial systems (which have also depressed savings); and, more recently, of changes in public sector savings (which have increased substantially in some countries in recent years).

By contrast, evidence from project countries suggests that the impact of capital flows on investment has been consistently positive, although varying considerably in degree. Although it is difficult to disentangle the effects of capital flows from those of other factors affecting the investment climate

— such as political stability, privatisation programmes, export retention schemes and the exchange rate regime — evidence from a variety of sources suggests that private flows, especially in the form of foreign direct investment, are highly correlated with gross domestic investment.

One issue that emerges is the nature of causality in this relationship. It is possible that increased inflows stimulate higher domestic investment. But, it is also possible that rises in domestic investment attract higher levels of FDI. Finally, changes in other factors — such as interest rates and rates of return more generally as well as other aspects of the economic and policy environment — may cause both domestic and foreign investment to change. There is evidence supportive of each of these three possibilities for at least some of the countries as well as evidence, particularly from South Africa, that the nature of causality in the relationship has been different in different periods.

Evidence of a positive relationship between capital inflows and growth is also found in many countries. The role of external savings in financing investment is identified as important as are the transfers of technology and technical and managerial skills associated with FDI. There are also specific factors such as access to coffee prefinance from foreign sources, which was critical in Uganda.

Monetary policy and real interest rates. The rise in capital flows in the 1990s has had a profound impact on monetary conditions, monetary policy and financial markets in all the project countries. The rise in capital flows has been associated with concerted programmes of financial liberalisation and macroeconomic stabilisation, the result of which has been a profound structural change in the macroeconomic environment. Moreover, as a result of the increase in international capital flows, changes in net foreign assets have become a more important — and, in many cases, dominant — determinant of changes in the money supply. Capital flows influence inflation and the macroeconomy through their effects not only on interest rates, but also on exchange rates. Finally, the increasing volatility of capital flows that has accompanied the rising levels has had implications for monetary conditions and for financial markets more generally.

The combination of financial liberalisation, a broad commitment to maintaining macroeconomic stability and an increase in private capital flows has led to a sea change in the level of real interest rates throughout the region. Virtually without exception, financial liberalisation and macroeconomic stabilisation led to a sharp upwards jump in real interest rates, which had been negative through much of the 1980s and now became significantly positive. The unexpected persistence of high real interest rates, in most countries, has raised questions throughout the region concerning the potential costs associated with the new openness to private capital flows. In countries where capital markets are deepest, such as South Africa, the importance of capital flows and changes in foreign (especially US) interest rates in determining domestic interest rates is readily apparent.

The effects of capital flows on interest rates depend importantly on the policy stance adopted by the authorities, as discussed further below. In countries such as Tanzania and Uganda, where concerns about macroeconomic stability have led the authorities to allow an appreciation of the real exchange rate, capital flows have had more limited effects on domestic interest rates. In Zimbabwe, there is evidence of a strong causal link between capital inflows and interest rates. In South Africa, the discount rate system of monetary policy that was followed until early 1998 meant that short term interest rates were unresponsive to capital flows, but long-term interest rates moved sharply, largely as a result of the actions of foreign investors in the bond market. Since March 1998, when the authorities shifted to a repo tender system for monetary policy, short-term interest rates have become much more responsive to changing capital flows.

A second important channel by which capital flows have had an impact on monetary conditions, and hence inflationary pressures, is via effects on the exchange rate. Rising exchange rates have acted to slow the economy during periods of capital inflows, although the divergent inflationary experiences of Uganda and Tanzania in 1994-5 underscore the continued importance of the fiscal stance.

Financial market volatility. Assessing the impact of capital flows on financial market volatility in Africa is difficult, as virtually every country has been engaged in liberalisation programmes which have focussed, in part, on shifting from administered prices to more market-determined prices. As a result, the increased volatility which can be observed in both exchange rates and interest rates in the recent period is, in part, a product of these reforms. Nevertheless, the analysis in the country studies suggests that capital flows have increased volatility. Although Africa has, to date, escaped the acute financial instability experienced in Mexico in 1994-5 and in Asia in 1997-8, the narrow, illiquid markets found in most countries are ill-suited to the task of absorbing the large swings in capital flows that have occurred in recent years. The non-existence or narrowness of capital markets, in particular, may make these countries more vulnerable to asset price bubbles and the associated risk of crashes. Even in South Africa, with the deepest and most liquid capital markets in the region, the swings in capital flows experienced since 1994 have led to heightened volatility in both interest rates and the exchange rate.

8.7 Policy Responses

A key determinant of the ultimate balance between the positive and negative macroeconomic effects identified in Chapter 6 is the set of strategies adopted by governments in response to private capital flows. Where capital flows are large — as they have been, at least in some recent years, for all of the countries studied here — such strategies are likely to prove crucial to limiting the destabilising effects of capital inflows, while at the same time not eroding the higher growth rates and investment that can result.

While achieving certain macroeconomic or other objectives may represent the primary justification for government intervention, governments increasingly recognise that they may have an implicit (or even explicit) liability for servicing private capital flows. The Asian crisis of 1997-8 makes it clear that this liability constitutes a powerful argument for governments to adopt an active and broad-ranging approach in responding to cross-border private capital flows. All of these factors feed into the policy choices in the project countries, where authorities tend to focus on containing vulnerability to possible flow reversals, and minimising risks of overheating, excessive real exchange rate appreciation, and unsustainable consumption growth.

Appropriate policy responses depend on the availability and flexibility of various policy instruments, the nature of domestic financial markets, the scale and composition of inflows, the prevailing policy environment and the extent of policymakers' credibility. While, in theory, policy responses should also be guided by the causes of flows, evidence from our project countries shows that the causes of capital flows are difficult to identify in practice.

Policy options have embraced foreign exchange market intervention, capital account liberalisation, monetary policy and sterilisation, fiscal policy, and financial sector reform and development.

Foreign exchange market intervention and exchange rate policy. Faced by surges in capital inflows and outflows, the most immediate challenge posed to the authorities in these countries is how best to manage the exchange rate and foreign reserves. In particular, the authorities have to decide whether, or to what extent, to allow an appreciation of the exchange rate. The alternative is to allow an accumulation of foreign exchange reserves so as to limit appreciation.

In the 1980s, many African countries were effectively operating some form of fixed exchange rate regime — although typically in a situation of multiple exchange rates as a result of the emergence of parallel foreign exchange markets. By the mid-1990s, most — including all five countries studied here — had succeeded in unifying the foreign exchange market and, in the process, had shifted to some kind of floating regime. While an important motivation for this shift was volatility of the balance of payments — due, in part, to volatile private capital flows — the expected benefits in the form of greater independence in setting domestic interest rates have failed to materialise. Indeed, the recent experience in Africa seems to mirror that in Latin America, where Hausmann *et al* (1999) find that flexible exchange rates have, in fact, resulted in higher real interest rates and increased sensitivity of domestic rates to changes in international interest rates. These tentative findings are far from conclusive, but suggest that the question of the appropriate exchange rate regime for developing countries in Africa remains very much open.

African countries have opted not for "pure" floating exchange rate regimes, but instead for the common intermediate case of a "managed" float — in which the authorities must decide on the appropriate trade-off between an appreciation of the currency and an accumulation of foreign reserves. While allowing the exchange rate to appreciate may facilitate foreign debt service and help contain inflationary pressures, allowing an increase in foreign reserves (to limit the exchange rate rise) may be important to mitigate the deterioration in competitiveness, which can undermine export promotion efforts. The strategies adopted in making these trade-offs have, inevitably, differed across countries and over time. Moreover, the volatility of capital flows has led governments also to intervene with the objective of smoothing inflows and outflows.

Concerns about potentially destabilising inflationary pressures, combined with limited capacity for sterilisation, has meant that capital inflows have, in most cases, been associated with significant appreciation of the exchange rate — leading to widespread concerns about the implications for competitiveness.

South Africa's approach has differed from others primarily in the greater scope for intervention afforded by its more developed financial markets. Two features of South Africa's intervention strategy are particularly noteworthy. First, the Reserve Bank has made heavy use of forward transactions both to alter the supply of dollars to the foreign exchange market (without affecting gross or net foreign reserves) and to alter its own (spot) foreign exchange reserves. While forward market intervention has dramatically enhanced the Bank's ability to dampen volatility in foreign exchange markets, the availability of such a "deep pocket" for intervention has created an incentive to intervene excessively. Second, the Reserve Bank has complemented its intervention in the spot and forward foreign exchange markets with what might be called "potential" intervention in the form of signals of its ability and willingness to intervene. In particular, it has used international credit lines — that is, potential borrowed reserves — as an instrument for influencing the foreign exchange markets via the expectations of market participants.

Capital account liberalisation. While foreign exchange intervention and sterilisation measures (discussed below) focus on mitigating the adverse effects of capital flows, countries have used capital account liberalisation, and related measures, to alter the level or composition of the flows themselves. Liberalisation of controls on non-residents has contributed to increased inflows — although sometimes, as in Zambia, a pent-up demand for foreign exchange has initially led to outflows. Liberalisation of controls on residents has been used, especially in South Africa, to help offset excessive foreign capital inflows by increasing outflows by residents. Lifting controls on residents can also, however, stimulate inflows by facilitating the return of flight capital, as shown by the experiences of Uganda and Tanzania.

While the focus throughout Africa has, to date, been on the liberalisation of capital controls used historically to protect the balance of payments, authorities are increasingly considering the potential role of measures such as the taxation of inflows and special reserve requirements on foreign credits as possibly valuable instruments for managing more effectively the composition and level of foreign inflows — and their macroeconomic impact. The Asian crisis clearly illustrated how capital controls have provided a regulatory function that goes far beyond the protection of the balance of payments. The challenge now facing countries throughout Africa is how best to ensure that mechanisms are in place, once exchange controls are lifted, to limit the systemic risk associated with foreign exchange transactions by resident banks and companies.

The sequencing, timing, speed, consistency and credibility of reforms are also critical issues. The regulatory roles that have implicitly been performed by capital controls indicate that early liberalisation of the capital account may have a devastating impact on the financial sector.

One of the most striking findings to emerge from the country studies is the extent to which current account liberalisation led to a *de facto* liberalisation of the capital account. This is most evident in the experience of Uganda and Tanzania, and evidence on capital flight from South Africa suggests a similar pattern.

The project countries have differed markedly in the timing and sequencing of liberalisation of the capital account — with some, including Zambia and Uganda, opting for a "big bang" approach, while others, notably South Africa and Zimbabwe, have opted for a gradual, phased approach. While the reforms adopted by those following the "big bang" approach have been sustained, the experiences of the project countries following the gradual approach have been mixed. The reforms in South Africa have been sustained and further developed — despite several periods of acute balance of payments pressure. In Zimbabwe, by contrast, balance of payments pressures led, in 1998, to a reversal of reforms. These divergent experiences suggest that gradual approaches, to be successful, require a higher degree of credibility on the part of the authorities. Where such credibility is lacking, the "big bang" approach has the advantage that it makes the reforms themselves more credible (by making them significantly more difficult and costly to reverse) — a factor that was explicitly recognised by the Zambian authorities.

It is, however, the phased approach to liberalisation as followed by South Africa that has been most successful in minimising the associated market and macroeconomic disruption. One of the lessons to emerge from the South African experience is the need for authorities to be attentive not only to the pace of liberalisation — taking care, for example, to spread the impact on the balance of payments wherever possible — but also to the sequencing of reforms (especially as regards the fiscal and regulatory framework) and to the need to manage private sector expectations in the lead up to reforms.

There has been some discussion within the project countries of the possible role of selective capital controls — such as special reserve requirements for foreign borrowing — to assist the authorities in managing the impact of capital flow surges. While it is clear from international experience that such controls are no substitute for sound monetary, fiscal and regulatory policy, they may be useful in helping to dampen volatile short-term capital movements and to reduce the costs of sterilisation. While, in theory, the case for such controls is strong, considerable practical difficulties currently impede their implementation in Africa. First, since special reserve requirements may be seen as a form of capital control, there is a risk that investors may perceive essentially prudent controls as policy reversals. This suggests that such controls are best introduced from a position of strength, when inflows are strong and government credibility is high. Second, the data on capital flows available to the authorities are weak, with serious problems of non-recorded flows and of misclassification. This second problem reinforces the arguments advanced above for governments to give high priority to increasing their ability to measure and monitor private capital movements.

Monetary policy. While fiscal adjustment and other policies form an important part of the medium-term policy response to capital flows, the macroeconomic policy response to capital flows has rested heavily on monetary policy. In particular, monetary policy has been the primary instrument, alongside exchange rate policy, for the short-term management of the macroeconomic impact of such flows.

Attempts to limit the upward pressure on the exchange rate in situations of large capital inflows have inevitably resulted in an increase in the central bank's net holdings of foreign assets. The challenge then facing the authorities has been how to sterilise these flows by managing the central bank's balance sheet so as to avoid an excessive monetary expansion (or contraction, in the case of large outflows).

The scope for sterilisation in most African countries is, however, severely circumscribed by the relatively undeveloped state of securities markets. This means, in turn, that the scope for managing the macroeconomic impact of capital flow surges is also severely limited. Either authorities allow the exchange rate to appreciate or they engage in unsterilised foreign exchange intervention — leading to reserves accumulation, increases in the money supply and inflationary pressures. In both cases, the net effect is an increase in the real exchange rate (the first involving a rise in the nominal exchange rate, the second a rise in inflation).

Uganda, for example, has had minimal success in containing monetary growth through monetary policy in a liberalised financial system, and the problem of thin and underdeveloped financial markets has been aggravated by distressed banking systems and other factors. Problems such as these have placed increasing pressure on fiscal policy, as discussed below, but they also highlight the need for continued emphasis on financial market development.

An important exception to this widespread pattern is South Africa, where market (and non-market) oriented monetary measures have been employed with considerable success to manage the macroeconomic impact of capital inflows and outflows. While the authorities have made use of open market operations in government securities, the dominant market-oriented instrument has been foreign exchange swaps.

The quasi-fiscal costs of open market operations (including swaps) can be high — as the interest differential between the high yield domestic bonds that authorities are, in effect, substituting for low-yield foreign exchange is substantial for every African country — and their effectiveness is set to diminish as financial liberalisation and technological change increasingly link domestic and international financial markets. Nevertheless, the South African experience highlights the important role that such operations can play in limiting the adverse macroeconomic effects of swings in capital flows.

Non-market operations have also played an important role in liquidity management in response to swings in international capital flows. Transfers of public sector deposits have been considered in several countries, but only used to any extent in South Africa. Even there, the use has now all but ended as government efforts to improve cash management have eliminated the "idle" balances previously used for such transfers.

The most widely used non-market instrument throughout Africa has been changes in reserve requirements. In many countries, such changes have been used heavily as an instrument of sterilisation. During the 1994-95 coffee boom, for example, Tanzania raised the cash reserve requirement eight times to drain excess liquidity from the banking sector. Zimbabwe, too, has used changes in reserve requirements to manage the impact of destabilising capital flows.

It is, however, increasingly recognised that heavy use of such requirements can work against financial development. By acting as a tax on bank intermediation, reserve requirements can induce savers and borrowers to shift to non-bank financial institutions with adverse implications for monetary control, regulation and supervision and efficiency. That said, it is also recognised that the more effective targeting of such requirements — for example, on off-shore borrowing by banks or on new borrowing after a certain date — may make such requirements substantially more effective in achieving policy objectives while creating significantly less distortion to intermediation generally.

Finally, it is important to note that the sharp increases in the level and volatility of capital flows have had implications for monetary policy frameworks throughout the region. Money supply targets have been downgraded, while the range of intermediate targets used has been broadened, with the exchange rate playing a more important role.

Fiscal policy. After exchange rate policy, fiscal policy has arguably been the most important policy instrument used by African countries in response to changing capital flows. Faced by severe constraints on the scope for using monetary policy, the authorities have attempted to mitigate the adverse macroeconomic impact of capital inflows by decreasing the government's own contribution to the expansion of domestic liquidity. The principal difficulty with this approach has been that raising additional revenue is not easy, especially where the formal sector is already heavily taxed, and cutting expenditure can have adverse social consequences.

At least as important as its impact on domestic liquidity has been the role of fiscal policy as a signal of governments' commitment to macroeconomic stability. In this regard, success in reducing large fiscal deficits has, throughout Africa, often proved important in attracting capital inflows — and in stemming capital outflows.

A salient feature of the role of fiscal policy in macroeconomic stabilisation in the project countries has been the importance of institutional reforms. One example has been the high profile and successful crackdown on tax evasion which has boosted revenues in Zimbabwe since 1997. Another has been the enhancement of expenditure control in South Africa through adoption of a medium-term expenditure framework A third example has been the adoption of cash budgets in Tanzania and Zambia, with dramatic effects on deficits and inflation. Finally, a number of countries, including South Africa, Tanzania, Uganda and Zambia, have increased revenues as a result of granting the revenue authorities a substantial degree of autonomy — although the mixed subsequent experiences in the latter three countries indicate that institutional reform alone is no panacea. One of the important characteristics of institutional reforms such as these is that by making policy reversals more visible and costly, they work to enhance the credibility of governments' commitment to reform.

Financial sector development. One of the lessons to emerge from the crises in Latin America and in Asia is the crucial importance of effective banking regulation and supervision in making financial systems — and economies — more robust to swings in private capital flows. Surges in capital inflows increase the level of non-performing assets, thereby increasing the vulnerability to flow reversals.

Raising the quality of financial regulation and, on the part of the private sector, of risk management is today a daunting task for even the most developed economies, and one that can easily outstrip the skills and expertise available in the developing countries of Africa. A promising development in many of the project countries has been the increasing role of "imported" risk management skills — and even regulation. Where the licensing of new, international banks has been well-handled, the result has been an influx of managerial and technical expertise in risk management with benefits for the financial system as a whole. In addition, domestic regulators have often, in such cases, benefited from closer relationships with the international banks' "lead regulators". But these benefits may be hard to realise. The collapse of foreign banks — as with BCCI and Meridien — can undermine domestic banking systems as can the wholesale capture of profitable niche markets by foreign banks.

Apart from regulatory issues, capital flows have also, for all the project countries, accelerated the agenda for financial sector development in other dimensions, notably the pressure to develop capital markets (especially stock exchanges) as a vehicle for the efficient allocation of inflowing capital. Many of the countries in the region have given high priority to establishing the legal and institutional framework for capital markets. In Zambia, a stock exchange was established in 1992 and in Tanzania, as discussed above, the framework for capital markets was set out in 1994 and the Dar-es-Salaam Stock Exchange was established.

Bibliography

Africa Financing Review (various issues), especially November 1996.

African Development Bank (1993), *Economic Integration in Southern Africa Vol. 2*, ADB.

African Review (1996), August.

Alile, H.I. and A.R. Anao (1986), *The Nigerian Stock Market in Operation*, Nigerian Stock Exchange, Lagos.

Anglo American Corporation of South Africa Limited (1996), *Annual Report and Chairman's Statement*, Johannesburg.

Aron, J. and I. Elbadawi (forthcoming), *Reflections on the South African Rand Crisis of 1996 and Policy Consequences*, World Bank, Washington, D.C.

Asea, P.K. and C.M. Reinhart (1995), "Real Interest Rate Differentials and the Real Exchange Rate: Evidence from Four African Countries", paper to an AERC workshop, Nairobi, June.

Bank for International Settlements (1995a), *Annual Report 1994/5*, Basle.

Bank for International Settlements (1995b), *International Banking and Financial Market Developments*, Basle.

Bank of England (1998), *Bank of England Banking Act Report 1997-8*, London, May.

Bennell, P. (1995), "British Manufacturing Investment in Sub-Saharan Africa: Corporate Responses During Structural Adjustment", In: *Journal of Development Studies*, Vol.32, No.2, pp.195-217, December.

Bhattacharya, A., P. Montiel and S. Sharma (1996), "Private Capital Flows to Sub-Saharan Africa: An Overview of Trends and Determinants", draft, 5 December.

Bhinda, N. and L. Thomas (1998), "Monitoring Private Capital Flows in Eastern and Southern Africa", In: *CREFSA Quarterly Review*, Vol. 3.

Bhinda, N. and M. Martin (1997), *External Finance and Macroeconomic Policy in Eastern and Southern Africa: Senior Policy Seminar Report*, Cape Town, 16-18 July, 1997.

Bhinda, N., M. Martin and S. Griffith-Jones (1997), "Private Capital Flows to Sub-Saharan Africa: A Supply-Side Study".

Bouton, L. and M. Sumlinski (1997), *Trends in Private Investment in Developing Countries: Statistics for 1970-95*, IFC Discussion Paper Number 31, Revised Version, IFC, Washington, D.C., February.

Calvo, G. and E. Mendoza (1995), "Reflections on Mexico's Balance of Payments Crisis", mimeo, University of Maryland, October.

Calvo, G., L. Leiderman and C. Reinhart (1993), *The Capital Flows Problem: Concepts and Issues*, IMF Paper on Policy Analysis and Assessment, PPA/93/10, IMF, Washington, D.C.

Calvo, G., L. Leiderman and C. Reinhart (1991), *The Perils of Sterilisation*, IMF Staff Papers, Vol. 38, No. 4, IMF, Washington, D.C., December, pp.151-174.

Chuhan, P., S. Claessens and N. Mamingi (1993), *Equity and Bond Flows to Latin America and Asia: the Role of Global and Country Factors*, World Bank/IECIF Policy Research Working Paper No.1160, World Bank, Washington, D.C., July.

Corbo, V. and L. Hernandez (1994), *Macroeconomic Adjustment to Capital Inflows: Latin American Style Versus East Asian Style*, World Bank/IECIF Policy Research Working Paper No.1377, World Bank, Washington, D.C., November.

Dindoyal, S. (1998), "Mauritius Stock Exchange Commission", Presentation to the EFA-CREFSA Workshop on Monitoring Private Capital Flows in Eastern and Southern Africa, Pretoria, 27-29 July.

Dornbusch, R. (1997), "Cross Border Payments Taxes and Alternative Capital Account Regimes", In: UNCTAD, *International Monetary and Financial Issues for the 1990s*, Vol.8, UNCTAD/GID/G24/8, United Nations, New York and Geneva, pp. 27-35.

Economist Intelligence Unit Country Risk Service (1998), *December Handbook 1998*, EIU, London.

Economist Intelligence Unit Country Risk Service (various issues), *Main Reports for South Africa, Tanzania, Uganda, Zambia, Zimbabwe*, 1st and 3rd quarters, 1997-1998, EIU, London.

Economist Intelligence Unit Country Risk Service (1996), *December Handbook 1996*, EIU, London.

Economist Intelligence Unit Country Risk Service (various issues), *Risk Ratings Review*, quarterly reports 1992-1996, EIU, London.

Emenuga, C. (1997), "Development of Stock Markets in Sub-Saharan Africa", In: *African Development Review*, Vol. 9, No. 1, June, pp. 156-185.

Emerging Market Investor (various issues), particularly June 1996.

Euromoney (various issues), 1992-98.

External Finance for Africa (1997), *Capital Flows and Macroeconomic Policy in Eastern And Southern Africa: Final Report to Funders*, 25 March, EFA, London.

External Finance for Africa (1996), *Financing Imports for Development in Low Income Africa*, EFA, London.

External Finance for Africa (1993), *How Much Aid Does Africa Need?*, EFA, London.

External Finance for Africa and Centre for Research into Economics and

Finance in Southern Africa (1998), *Monitoring Private Capital Flows in Eastern and Southern Africa: Report to Donors*, London.

External Finance for Africa and Centre for Research into Economics and Finance in Southern Africa (1997), *Intra-regional Private Capital Flows in Eastern and Southern Africa: Project Proposal*, London.

External Finance for Africa and Centre for Research into Economics and Finance in Southern Africa (1997), *Monitoring Private Capital Flows in Eastern and Southern Africa: Project Proposal*, London.

Fernandez-Arias, E. (1994), *The New Wave of Private Capital Inflows: Push or Pull?*, World Bank/IECIF Policy Research Working Paper No. 1312, Washington D.C., June.

Fischer, B. and H. Reisen (1992), *Towards Capital Account Convertibility*, OECD Policy Brief No.4, Paris.

Griffith-Jones, S. (1998), *Global Capital Flows*, Macmillan.

Griffith-Jones, S. (1996), "Study of Movement of Funds on the Global Market", paper prepared for Grupo de Analise e Pesquisa, Presidencia de Republica Brazil, Institute for Development Studies, Sussex.

Griffith-Jones, S. (1995), "Capital Flows to Latin America and Asia: Lessons for Eastern Europe", mimeo, Institute for Development Studies, Sussex, June.

Hall, R. (1988), "Intertemporal substitution in consumption", In: *Journal of Political Economy 96*, no. 2 (April), pp.339-357.

Haque, N.U., M.S. Kumar, N. Mark and D.J. Mathieson (1996), *The Economic Content of Indicators of Developing Country Creditworthiness*, IMF Working Paper WP/96/9, IMF, Washington, D.C.

Hausmann, R., M. Gavin, C. Pages-Serra and E. Stein (1999), *Financial Turmoil and the Choice of Exchange Rate Regime*, Office of the Chief Economist, InterAmerican Development Bank.

Helleiner, G.K. (1997), "Capital Account Regimes and the Developing Countries", In: UNCTAD, *International Monetary and Financial Issues for the 1990s*, Vol.8, UNCTAD/GID/G24/8, United Nations, New York and Geneva, pp. 1-25.

Helleiner, G.K. (1996), "Private Capital Flows and Development: the Role of National and International Policies", mimeo.

IBCA *Ratings* (various issues), particularly September 1996.

International Finance Corporation (1998), *Emerging Stockmarkets Factbook 1998*, IFC, Washington, D.C.

International Finance Corporation (1997), *Annual Report*, IFC, Washington, D.C.

International Finance Corporation (1996), *Emerging Stockmarkets Factbook 1996*, IFC, Washington, D.C.

International Monetary Fund (1997), *Balance of Payments Statistics Yearbook 1997*, Washington, D.C.

International Monetary Fund (1996a), *World Economic Outlook*, IMF, Washington, D.C.

International Monetary Fund (1996b), *International Capital Market Report*, IMF, Washington, D.C.

International Monetary Fund (1996c), *Balance of Payments Textbook*, IMF, Washington, D.C.

International Monetary Fund (1996d), *Coordinated Portfolio Investment Survey: Survey Guide*, IMF, Washington, D.C.

International Monetary Fund (1996e), *Balance of Payments Compilation Guide*, IMF, Washington, D.C.

International Monetary Fund (1995), *International Capital Markets: Developments, Prospects and Policy Issues*, IMF, Washington D.C.

International Monetary Fund (1993), *Balance of Payments Manual* 5th *Edition*, IMF, Washington, D.C.

International Monetary Fund (1977), *Balance of Payments Manual* 4th *Edition*, IMF, Washington, D.C.

Institutional Investor (various issues), 1992-98.

Jaspersen, F., A. Aylward and M. Sumlinski (1996), *Trends in Private Investment in Developing Countries: Statistics for 1970-94*, IFC Discussion Paper Number 28, Washington, D.C.

Jefferis, K.R., C.C. Okeahalam and T.T. Matome (1997), "International Stock Market Linkages in Southern Africa", Final Research Report submitted to AERC Research Workshop, Harare, November.

Jenkins, C. and L. Thomas (1999), "The Macroeconomic Policy Framework", In: C. Jenkins *et al* (eds.), *Gaining from Free Trade in Southern Africa: Complementary Policies to Support the SADC Free Trade Area*, Macmillan, forthcoming.

Kahn, B. and J. Leape (1997), "South African Exchange Control Reform: An Update", In: *Quarterly Review*, Centre for Research into Economics and Finance in Southern Africa, London School of Economics, July.

Kahn, B. and J. Leape (1996), "Managing the Rand's Depreciation: The Role of Intervention", In: *Quarterly Review*, Centre for Research into Economics and Finance in Southern Africa, London School of Economics, April.

Kasekende, L. and D. Kitabire (1997), "Capital Flows Study: Uganda", paper presented to EFA Workshop on Private Capital Flows and Macroeconomic Policy in Sub-Saharan Africa, Cape Town, 15-15 July.

Kasekende, L., D. Kitabire and M. Martin (1996), "Capital Inflows and Macroeconomic Policy in Sub-Saharan Africa", In: UNCTAD, *International Monetary and Financial Issues for the 1990s*, Vol.8,

UNCTAD/GID/G24/8, United Nations, New York and Geneva, pp. 59-85.

Kasekende, L. and M. Martin (1995), "Macroeconomic Policy Research Issues: The Sequencing, Credibility and Consistency of Adjustment in Africa", paper presented at an African Economic Consortium Senior Policy Seminar, Nairobi, April.

Khatri, Y., and J. Leape (1997), "The South-East Asian Crisis and Implications for South Africa", *Quarterly Review*, Centre for Research into Economics and Finance in Southern Africa, London School of Economics, October.

Khatri, Y., J. Leape and E. van der Merwe (1997), "Capital Flows and Macroeconomic Policy in South Africa", paper presented to EFA Workshop on Private Capital Flows and Macroeconomic Policy in Sub-Saharan Africa, Cape Town, 15-15 July.

Kimei, C., G.D. Mjema, B. Tarimo and A. Msutze (with M. Martin and N. Bhinda) (1997), "Tanzania: Capital Flows Study", paper presented to EFA Workshop on Private Capital Flows and Macroeconomic Policy in Sub-Saharan Africa, Cape Town, 15-15 July.

Kufeni, S., R. Mkwebu and M. Mpofu (1997), "Private Capital Flows and Macroeconomic Policy in Zimbabwe", paper presented to EFA Workshop on Private Capital Flows and Macroeconomic Policy in Sub-Saharan Africa, Cape Town, 15-15 July.

Jenkins, C., J. Leape and L. Thomas (eds.) (1999), *Gaining From Trade in Southern Africa: Complementary Policies to Support the SADC Free Trade Area*, Macmillan, forthcoming.

Leape, J. (1999), "Taxation and Fiscal Adjustment", In: Jenkins *et al* (eds.), *Gaining From Trade in Southern Africa: Complementary Policies to Support the SADC Free Trade Area*, Macmillan, forthcoming.

Leape, J. (1998a), "Macroeconomic Policy Responses to Capital Flows", In: *Quarterly Review*, Centre for Research into Economics and Finance in Southern Africa, London School of Economics, 1998 no.1.

Leape, J. (1998b), "Strategic Issues in Methodology", Presentation to the EFA-CREFSA Workshop on Monitoring Private Capital Flows in Eastern and Southern Africa, Pretoria, 27-29 July.

Leape, J. (1991), *South Africa's Foreign Debt and the Standstill, 1985-1990*, Research Paper No. 1, Centre for Research into Economics and Finance in Southern Africa, London School of Economics.

Lee, J. (1996), *Implications of A Surge in Capital Inflows: Available Tools and Consequences for the Conduct of Monetary Policy*, IMF Working Paper, WP/96/53, IMF, Washington, D.C.

Levine, R. and S. Zervos (1996), *Stock Market Development and Long-Run Growth*, Policy Research Working Paper no. 1582, The World Bank,

March.

Lofchie, M. and T. Callaghy (1995), "Diversity in the Tanzanian Business Community: its Implications for Economic Growth", draft version for USAID, 20 November.

London Economics (1996), "Costs and Benefits Associated with Commercial Debt Buy Back Operations in SSA", mimeo, Report to ODA, July.

Martin, M. and N. Bhinda (1998), "Monitoring Private Capital Flows in Eastern and Southern Africa", Background Technical Paper to the EFA-CREFSA Workshop, Pretoria, 27-29 July.

Martin, M., S. Griffith-Jones, L. Kasekende and D. Kitabire (1995), *Capital Flows and Macroeconomic Policy in Eastern and Southern Africa*, Project Document to SIDA and Danish Foreign Ministry, External Finance for Africa, December.

Matale, A., I. Mwanawina, J. Matale and J. Mweetwa (1997), "Capital Inflows and Macroeconomic Policy in Zambia", paper presented to EFA workshop on Private Capital Flows and Macroeconomic Policy in Sub-Saharan Africa, Cape Town, 15-15 July.

Mathieson, D.J. and L. Rojas-Suarez (1993), *Liberalisation of the Capital Account: Experiences and Issues*, IMF Occasional Paper, No.103, IMF, Washington, D.C., March.

Mauritius Fund Management Company Limited (1996), *Shareholders Bulletin for December 1996*.

MEFMI (1997), "Project Proposal on Private Debt".

Merchant International Group (1999), *The Intelligence Gap 1999*, MIG.

Micropal Emerging Market Fund Monitor (various issues).

Mistry, P. (1996), "Regional Dimensions of Structural Adjustment in Southern Africa", In: J.J. Teunissen (ed.), *Regionalism and the Global Economy: The Case of Africa*, FONDAD, The Hague.

Mistry, P. and S. Griffith-Jones (1993), *Debt Conversion for Low-Income Countries*, UNCTAD.

Mkwebu, R. and M. Mpofu (1998), "Monitoring External Sector Private Debt Flows in Zimbabwe", Reserve Bank of Zimbabwe, Presentation to the EFA-CREFSA Workshop on Monitoring Private Capital Flows in Eastern and Southern Africa, Pretoria, 27-29 July.

Moody's, various press releases and publications.

Ncube, M., J. Leape and L. Thomas (1996), "The Internationalisation of South Africa's Securities Markets: An Overview", In: *Quarterly Review*, Centre for Research into Economics and Finance in Southern Africa, London School of Economics, October 1996.

N'Guessan, T. (1997), "Reforme des Institutions Financières Non-Bancaires, Mobilisation et Allocation des Resources Domestiques: Le Cas de la BVA", paper prepared for the second AERC Senior Policy Seminar, Abidjan.

Njinkeu, D. (1997), "Impact of Banking Sector Reforms in Francophone Africa", paper prepared for the second AERC Senior Policy Seminar, Abidjan.

Obstfeld, M. (1995), *International Currency Experience: New Lessons and Lessons Relearned*, Brookings Papers on Economic Activity, No.1, Washington, D.C.

OECD / BIS, *Statistics on External Indebtedness: Bank and Trade-Related Non-Bank Claims on Individual Borrowing Countries and Territories*, various issues.

OECD (1992), *Detailed Benchmark Definitions of FDI*.

Pfeffermann, G. (1996), "Low Income Countries: Prospects for Increasing Capital Inflows: Focus on FDI", paper presented at World Bank/IMF Conference on External Financing for Low Income Countries, 10-11 December.

Reinhart, C.M. and S. Dunaway (1995), "Dealing with Capital Inflows: Are There Any Lessons?", mimeo, April.

Reisen, H. (1996), "Managing Volatile Capital Inflows: the Experience of the 1990s", In: *Asian Development Review*, Vol.14, No.1.

Riddell, R. and L. Cockcroft (1991), "Foreign Direct Investment", In: Husain, I. and J. Underwood (eds.), *African External Finance in the 1990s: A World Bank Symposium*, World Bank, Washington, D.C.

Sajjabi, D. and D. Ddamulira (1998), "The Foreign Exchange Market and Capital Flows to Uganda", Bank of Uganda Presentation to the EFA-CREFSA Workshop on Monitoring Private Capital Flows in Eastern and Southern Africa, Pretoria, 27-29 July.

Schadler, S., M. Carkovic, A. Bennet and R. Kahn (1993), *Recent Experiences with Surges in Capital Inflows*, Occasional Paper 108, International Monetary Fund, Washington, D.C.

Scheun, H. (1998), "FDI Issues in Namibia", Bank of Namibia Presentation to the EFA- CREFSA Workshop on Monitoring Private Capital Flows in Eastern and Southern Africa, Pretoria, 27-29 July.

South African Reserve Bank (various issues), *Quarterly Bulletins*, especially June 1998.

Soyibo, A. (1997), "Banking Sector Reforms in Africa: Effects on Savings, Investment and Financial Development", paper prepared for the second AERC Senior Policy Seminar.

Standard and Poors, various press releases and publications.

UNCTAD (1998), *World Investment Report 1998*, United Nations, New York and Geneva.

UNCTAD (1997a), *World Investment Report 1997*, United Nations, New York and Geneva.

UNCTAD (1997b), *World Investment Directory: Africa 1996*, United Nations, New York and Geneva.

UNCTAD (1996), *World Investment Report 1996*, United Nations, New York and Geneva.

UNCTAD (1995a), *World Investment Report 1995*, United Nations, New York and Geneva.

UNCTAD (1995b), *FDI in Africa*, United Nations, New York and Geneva.

USAID Tanzania (1996), "The Investor Roadmap of Tanzania", draft report prepared by the Services Group, December.

van der Merwe, E. (1998) "The Macroeconomic Effects of Capital Flows", In: *Quarterly Review*, Centre for Research into Economics and Finance in Eastern and Southern Africa, London School of Economics, 1998, No.1.

Van Hulten, M. and M. Schuerman (1996), *Country Credit Ratings from Sub-Saharan Africa, or Perceptions on the Creditworthiness of a Poor Continent*, Global Coalition for Africa.

Williamson, J. (1994), "The Management of Capital Inflows", paper for IFC and the Government of India, mimeo, December.

World Bank (1998), *Global Development Finance 1998*, Volumes 1 and 2, World Bank, Washington D.C.

World Bank (1997a), *Private Capital Flows to Developing Countries: The Road to Financial Integration*, World Bank/Oxford University Press.

World Bank (1997b), *Global Development Finance 1997*, Volumes 1 and 2, World Bank, Washington D.C.

World Bank (1996), *World Debt Tables 1996*, Volume 1, World Bank, Washington D.C.

World Bank/IMF, *Emerging Markets*, issue of 30/9/96 (article by Patrick Smith), and June 1996.

World Equity (1997), February.

Other Publications by Fondad

Jan Joost Teunissen (ed.), **Regulatory and Supervisory Challenges in a New Era of Global Finance,** December 1998.
ISBN: 90-74208-14-2, 280 pages
The recent financial crisis in Asia has once again alerted the international community to the fragility of the global financial system and the serious consequences of enormous, rapid private capital flows. In this book, experts from around the world discuss the implications of financial crises in developing and transition countries. Yung Chul Park (Korea Institute of Finance) presents an up-to-date account of the effects of and remedies for financial crisis in Asia and elsewhere. Charles Wyplosz (Graduate Institute of International Studies) reviews the lessons learnt, and not yet learnt. Jack Boorman (IMF) reflects on the causes and consequences of the Asian crisis and suggests how the IMF, other creditors and the private sector should be involved in dealing with future crises. Ariel Buira (formerly with the Central Bank of Mexico) suggests an alternative approach to dealing with financial crises by e.g. the timely provision of sufficient IMF support. Susan Phillips (US Fed) dwells on sound international supervision. William White (BIS) discusses the role of the Bank for International Settlements in promoting financial stability, Amaret Sila-On (Financial Sector Restructuring Authority, Thailand) and György Szapáry (National Bank of Hungary) discuss specific financial issues in each of their countries. Christian Larraín (Chile) deals extensively with the challenges of banking supervision in developing economies.

Jan Joost Teunissen (ed.), **The Policy Challenges of Global Financial Integration,** June 1998.
ISBN: 90-74208-13-4, 128 pages.
One of the main features of the globalising economy is the surge of cross-border capital flows around the world in the form of portfolio as well as foreign direct investment. In this book, H. Johannes Witteveen (former Managing Director of the IMF), Stephany Griffith-Jones (IDS, Sussex), Zdeněk Drábek (WTO) and Percy Mistry (Oxford International) give their views on the current policy challenges facing the international financial community. Witteveen presents a broad, long-term perspective on globalisation; Griffith-Jones looks at the regulatory challenges of surges in capital flows for source countries; Drábek presents an advocacy paper for the envisaged and much-debated Multilateral Agreement on Investment; and Mistry gives an original and well-informed account of the challenges to national and international financial institutions posed by emerging markets.

Jan Joost Teunissen (ed.), **Regional Integration and Multilateral Cooperation in the Global Economy,** June 1998.
ISBN: 90-74208-12-6, 248 pages.
This book concludes a multi-volume series which explores how regional integration and multilateral cooperation can be promoted in a mutually reinforcing manner. It includes papers presented at a two-day conference in which scholars and policymakers from various national and international organisations examined the role of regional integration and multilateral cooperation in a globalising economy. Contributors to the volume are Ernest Aryeety, Robert Devlin, Mohamed A. El-Erian, Ricardo Ffrench-Davis, Björn Hettne, András Inotai, Mats Karlsson, Hans Peter Lankes, Charles P. Oman, Arvind Panagariya, Miria Pigato, Jan P. Pronk, Piritta Sorsa and Rosalind H. Thomas. In addition, the volume includes summaries of the floor discussions at the conference.

Jan Joost Teunissen (ed.), **Regionalism and the Global Economy: The Case of Central and Eastern Europe,** June 1997.
ISBN: 90-74208-11-8, 254 pages.
New opportunities for regional integration were presented to the countries of Central and Eastern Europe when they embarked on their transition to democratic market economies at the end of the 1980s. While the ultimate goal is that these countries become members of the EU, they are also engaged in sub-regional integration efforts, as the free trade agreements among the Baltics as well as among the Central European countries demonstrate. This volume includes contributions from Zdeněk Drábek, Miroslav Hrnčíř, András Inotai, Piritta Sorsa, Mark Allen, Franz-Lothar Altmann, Mats Karlsson, Ricardo Lago, Friedemann Müller, Joan Pearce, Roberto Rocha, Inna Šteinbuka, and Per Magnus Wijkman. It presents an encompassing analysis of Central and Eastern Europe's economic integration and the prospects for EU enlargement. It also includes the stimulating discussion from a two-day conference at the Czech National Bank.

Jan Joost Teunissen (ed.), **Regionalism and the Global Economy: The Case of Africa,** November 1996.
ISBN: 90-74208-10-X, 312 pages.
This book explores why most cooperation and integration arrangements in Africa have failed, and how regional integration could be made more successful. Outstanding economists from African as well as international institutions, such as the World Bank, the African Development Bank and the International Monetary Fund, provide an in-depth analysis of Africa's past

and future prospects for economic integration. It includes contributions from Ernest Aryeetey, Peter Robinson, William Lyakurwa, Percy Mistry, Sam Asante, Alieu Jeng, Louis Kasekende, Mohsin Khan, Gavin Maasdorp, Sindiso Ngwenya, Gene Tidrick, and Samuel Wangwe. The book is enriched by a vivid account of a two-day conference in which the research was discussed in a creative and frank manner. Questions addressed include: What form of regional cooperation would be most relevant in different parts of the continent? How can policies of national governments and international financial institutions be improved in design as well as implementation?

Percy S. Mistry, **Regional Integration Arrangements in Economic Development: Panacea or Pitfall?**, October 1996.
ISBN: 90-74208-08-8, 98 pages.
This study is written by one of the stimulating forces in Fondad's research project on regionalism and multilateralism, Indian economist and investment banker Percy S. Mistry. Earlier drafts served as a framework paper to guide and inspire the thinking of participants in Fondad conferences. Mistry reviews issues arising from experience with arrangements for regional economic cooperation and integration in developing and developed regions of the world. Given the plethora and complexity of the issues involved – ranging from trade, finance and monetary matters to institutional, social and political affairs – the author has chosen a broad approach. However, at various points Mistry also presents some of his more detailed insights and policy suggestions.

Percy S. Mistry, **Resolving Africa's Multilateral Debt Problem: A Response to the IMF and the World Bank,** September 1996.
ISBN: 90-74208-09-6, 70 pages.
Since 1993, public concern about the problem of the growing multilateral debt overhang of poor countries has increased. While the IMF and the World Bank have proposed a special debt initiative for the heavily indebted poor countries, Percy Mistry argues that a different approach is needed. He suggests compelling arguments for a new strategy to resolve the multilateral debt problem of poor countries in Africa (and elsewhere) and spells out a set of alternative principles and measures on which a new strategy should be based.

Jan Joost Teunissen (ed.), **Can Currency Crises Be Prevented or Better Managed? Lessons from Mexico,** June 1996.
ISBN 90-74208-07-X, 115 pages.
Private capital flows are playing a growing and crucial role in industrial as well as developing countries. They may promote economic development or suddenly disrupt economic order and create serious crises. Mexico's currency crisis of December 1994 is a recent example. Discussing both the origins of and the remedies for Mexico-style crises, this book provides profound insights into a problem which is of concern to policymakers and the public at large in many countries of the world. The book reports on in-depth discussion of both short-term and long-term proposals discussed by a group of highly experienced researchers and central bankers. It includes papers by Ariel Buira, Peter Kenen, Stephany Griffith-Jones, and a joint paper by Barry Eichengreen and Charles Wyplosz. Buira reviews the main hypotheses that have been advanced to explain the Mexican crisis. Kenen addresses the more general issue of how the disruption to national economies that results from fluctuations in cross-border flows can be minimised. Griffith-Jones considers the new features of recent and possible future currency crises. Wyplosz and Eichengreen draw out some lessons from exchange rate crises that have occurred over the last thirty years in a large number of industrial countries.

Jan Joost Teunissen (ed.), **Regionalism and the Global Economy: The Case of Latin America and the Caribbean,** November 1995.
ISBN: 90-74208-06-1, 163 pages.
Many books and articles have appeared on the topic of regional integration in Latin America and the Caribbean, yet the debate is far from concluded. There is not only a lack of consensus but also a lack of factual information on important aspects. By focusing the research primarily on financial issues and by reporting extensively on a two-day discussion between experienced researchers and policymakers which was held at the Economic Commission for Latin America and the Caribbean in Santiago de Chile, this book hopes to make a contribution to both providing new information and shaping new opinions. The four papers presented in this volume are written by well-known experts Percy Mistry, Stephany Griffith-Jones, Ricardo Ffrench-Davis, and Roberto Bouzas. Mistry presents a thought-provoking and broad view of the problem; Griffith-Jones explores the little-researched financial aspects of Latin American integration; Ffrench-Davis focuses on the crucial role of intra-regional trade; Bouzas looks at the policy dilemmas and prospects posed by NAFTA.

Percy S. Mistry, **Multilateral Development Banks: An Assessment of their Financial Structures, Policies and Practices,** February 1995. ISBN: 90-74208-05-3, 308 pages.
As development agencies, multilateral development banks (MDBs) have received the greatest attention for their lending policies, for their technical assistance and advisory functions and, more recently, for their policy reform and adjustment prescriptions. Since the 1980s, they have become important instruments of economic and political governance over the developing world instead of being simply international financial intermediaries. However, very little is known publicly about their financial policies and operations. This book attempts to render understandable to those who are not financial experts, the main financial policies and practices of the MDBs as well as the implications and consequences of those policies and practices.

Percy S. Mistry, **Multilateral Debt: An Emerging Crisis?,** February 1994. ISBN: 90-74208-04-5, 76 pages.
This study is the first in-depth analysis of a problem which is of growing concern to world financial policymakers. While most attention has been focused on the attempts to alleviate the burdens of both commercial and official bilateral debt of the countries affected, a new problem has emerged: the pyramiding of multilateral debt.

Jan Joost Teunissen (ed.), **The Pursuit of Reform: Global Finance and the Developing Countries,** 1993.
ISBN: 90-74208-03-7, 196 pages.
Against the background of the daily reports on the dynamic developments taking place in the world economy, Fondad invited a group of eminent scholars and policymakers to discuss the functioning of the international monetary and financial system — with particular reference to the developing world and Eastern Europe. The book includes four papers presented by Richard N. Cooper, Stephany Griffith-Jones, Peter B. Kenen, and John Williamson; other contributors include Ariel Buira, Mohamed A. El-Erian, Gerald K. Helleiner, Wim Kok, Richard Portes, Jan P. Pronk, and Kumiharu Shigehara.

Jan Joost Teunissen (ed.), **Fragile Finance: Rethinking the International Monetary System,** 1992.
ISBN: 90-74208-02-9, 132 pages.
This book seeks to revive the policy debate on the functioning of the world

financial system. It includes three thought-provoking papers presented by well-known experts, Stephany Griffith-Jones, Arjun Sengupta and John Williamson at an international workshop in The Hague and reports on the ensuing lively and in-depth debate by a group of eminent officials, private bankers, researchers and politicians.

Percy S. Mistry, **African Debt Revisited: Procrastination or Progress?**, November 1991.
ISBN: 90-74208-01-0, 84 pages.
African Debt Revisited is an authoritative and compelling study on Africa's problems with bilateral, multilateral and private creditors. It suggests to policymakers, bankers and legislators what they could do to resolve Africa's debt problem.

Order Form

Number of copies, title and price (in Dutch guilders and Euros)

( )   Private Capital Flows to Africa: Perception and Reality (NLG40.00/€18.15)
( )   Regulatory and Supervisory Challenges in a New Era of Global Finance (NLG47.50/€21.55)
( )   The Policy Challenges of Global Financial Integration (NLG30.00/€13.61)
( )   Regional Integration and Multilateral Cooperation in the Global Economy (NLG45.00/€20.42)
( )   Regionalism and the Global Economy: The Case of Central and Eastern Europe (NLG45.00/€20.42)
( )   Regionalism and the Global Economy: The Case of Africa (NLG47.50/€21.55)
( )   Regional Integration Arrangements in Economic Development: Panacea or Pitfall? (NLG25.00/€11.35)
( )   Resolving Africa's Multilateral Debt Problem: A Response to the IMF and the World Bank (NLG25.00/€11.35)
( )   Can Currency Crises Be Prevented or Better Managed? Lessons from Mexico (NLG25.00/€11.35)
( )   Regionalism and the Global Economy: The Case of Latin America and the Caribbean (NLG37.50/€17.02)
( )   Multilateral Development Banks: An Assessment of their Financial Structures, Policies and Practices (NLG47.50/€21.55)
( )   Multilateral Debt: An Emerging Crisis? (NLG15.00/€6.81)
( )   The Pursuit of Reform: Global Finance and the Developing Countries (NLG25.00/€11.35)
( )   Fragile Finance: Rethinking the International Monetary System (NLG15.00/€6.81)
( )   African Debt Revisited: Procrastination or Progress? (NLG10.00/€4.54)

Name . . . .

Address . . . .

City . . . . Postal Code . . . .

Country . . . .

Payment Options

☐ Please send an invoice.
☐ Please debit my credit card for the corresponding amount in Euros.

( ) Mastercard   ( ) Visa   ( ) JCB Card   ( ) Diner's Club   ( ) American Express

Name of Cardholder . . . .

Card number . . . . Expiry date . . . .

Signature